American Heritage
Poetry Collection

American Heritage Poetry Collection

American Progress, Painting by John Gast, 1872

LTC Roy E. Peterson
U.S. Army Retired
Military Intelligence and
Russian Foreign Area Officer

authorHOUSE®

AuthorHouse™
1663 Liberty Drive
Bloomington, IN 47403
www.authorhouse.com
Phone: 1-800-839-8640

Published by AuthorHouse   12/12/2012

ISBN: 978-1-4772-9728-5 (sc)
ISBN: 978-1-4772-9726-1 (hc)
ISBN: 978-1-4772-9727-8 (e)

Library of Congress Control Number: 2012923279

Any people depicted in stock imagery provided by Thinkstock are models, and such images are being used for illustrative purposes only.
Certain stock imagery © Thinkstock.

This book is printed on acid-free paper.

Books Authored by LTC Roy E. Peterson

Albert: The Cat That Thought He Could Fly (Juvenile)
American Attache in the Moscow Maelstrom (Cold War History)
American Heartland Poet (Poetry)
Between Darkness and Light (Poetry)
Fight of the Phoenix (Vietnam War History)
Guardian Angel: All My Tomorrows (Poetry)
Iron Ikon (Historical Fiction about US Foreign Commercial
    Officer Service/Diplomat/Foreign Service)
Magnetism to Marriage (PreMarriage Relationships)
Russian Romance (Historical Fiction about IBM Penetration of
    the Russian Far East)
Soviet Intelligence Process (Out of Print)

Books Planned by LTC Roy E. Peterson

American Agenda: Regeneration Blueprint (Politics)
Maturity: Mind Over Matter (Relationships)
Intelligence: Collection, Collation, and Communication
    (Government)
Order of the Delta Dragon (Historical Fiction)
Power of the Pentagon (History)
Precious Promises: Engagement Means Commitment
    (Relationships)
Victorville Visions: Development, Disappointment, and Drama
    (Historical Business Fiction)

TABLE OF CONTENTS

PART V   MY FAMILY

PART VI   MY MUSIC

PART VII   MY HISTORY AND LEGENDS

PART XI   MY MYSTICAL MOMENTS

PART XII   MY MEMORIES

PART XIII   MY THOUGHTS

PART XIV   ANIMAL CRACKERS

DEDICATION

American Heritage Poetry Collection
LTC Roy E. Peterson, January 2013

American Heritage Poetry Collection is dedicated:

To inventors and achievers,
To aspirers and believers,
To writers and their readers,
To the honest and good deeders.

To industrial manufacturers,
To entrepreneurs and lecturers,
To the nurses and to preachers.
To our parents and to teachers.

To the patriots and good soldiers,
To the life and character molders,
To the men who move the boulders,
To the younger and the older.

To the farmer and the fireman,
To the cleaners with the dustpan,
To the family and the clansman,
To the cook stirring in her saucepan.

Roy Peterson
Tucson, Arizona
January 2013

FOREWORD

The American Heritage Poetry Collection

This collection of poetry is as diverse as America and as thought provoking as the passionate people inhabiting its expansive borders. In the confines of this tome are combined fifty years of poetry, running from 1962 to 2012. I provided the dates of first writing on the majority of the poems and they incorporate the decades and gaps in writing in the later decades until personal rediscovery of the early years of love, romance, nature, and social critique matched by more recent reflections on past life and the approaching departure from my earthly home.

As most poets do, I found the need for a collected works edition. I used virtually every poem that I deemed worthy of inclusion in my life works volume from three volumes of poetry:

Between Darkness and Light: Coal Eyes and Fight for Right, is a focused collection of early works that were the basis for songs, readings, and personal presentations to friends and relatives.

Guardian Angel was my resurrection of poetic passion as I wrote a song for my son's wedding; historical figures and events of my second home, which was in the oilfields of West Texas; and introspective, reflective, and humorous poems sculpted in 2011 and early 2012.

American Heartland is being published at approximately the same time as this comprehensive American Heritage collection. Many of these poems were written with greater intensity after ruminating through the classics that I loved.

All three volumes are worthy of purchase not just for the poetry, but for the extensive and often humorous lists, witty sayings and proverbs with twists, and wisdom that is exuded throughout the volumes.

I may never return to preparing a full volume of poetry and anticipate being content to let this stand as my seminal work in the field.

PART I

MY COUNTRY

By Dawn's Early Light Painting by Edward Moran

AWAKE YOUNG EAGLES

By Roy E. Peterson (1976)

Awake young eagles! Rise and spread
Your wings of glory overhead.
Descend from mountain crevices,
And lend to us your services.

Tell your fathers strong and proud
That freedom cast aside its shroud
To join us on this foreign strand,
Where it was safe from monarch's hand.

From every craggy mountain top
Young eagles rise and naught can stop
Your daring exploits for the cause
Of Freedom's plea to form new laws.
Let's set for every man the right
Of trial by jury, not by might.
Let's build freedom's sacred house,
And give democracy a spouse.

A new breed will come to plow the land,
Cut down the wilderness by hand.
A strong and great and mighty man
Will be one called American.

FIGHT FOR RIGHT

By Roy E. Peterson (1965)

A great war now is facing us
Between the minds of men.
On every side are battle lines
Drawn by our so-called friends.

When we face the enemy
Will we be strong and true,
Or will we fall before them all
As they come rushing through.

"To arms," the bugle's sounded clear.
It's time to fight again,"
But now it's on a different scale,
It's for the minds of men.

Each night as I lie thinking
An angel comes to me
And says, "Go fight for what is right,
Be strong for liberty."

A golden crested eagle
Stares at me without fear
And says, ""God's might is all that's right,
Your calling's very clear.

I scooped my helmet quickly up,
And bade my love goodbye.
I said, I'm going to fight for what is right.
For freedom I may die."

It takes a man to give his life.
It takes a mighty man
To say, "I have to fight for what is right.
I'll serve as best I can."

And when this great war's over,
No matter where I'll lie,
I'll say, "I did my best to keep men free,
And now I'm proud to die."

Perhaps someday when life is o'er
My sweetheart I shall see.
I'll say, "My darling I was in the right.
I fought for liberty."

MAY OLD GLORY ALWAYS WAVE

By Roy E. Peterson (July 4th, 2012)

May Old Glory always wave
Above the tumult and the fray.
Honor heroes that were brave
Until the final Judgment Day.

Drape the caskets of the dead,
Fallen soldiers everywhere.
Symbol of the prayers we said
And the battles we all share.

May the haters of our land,
Desecrators, those who shame,
Be destroyed by Patriot hand
And no one recall their name.

May a thousand flags replace
Everyone the evil shred.
May the cowards that disgrace
Become the dust on which we tread.

Honor country and Old Glory
Give salute on Veteran's Day.
Tell the never ending story
God protect the American way.

REND THE NIGHT

Remembering My Army Service
By Roy E. Peterson (August 24, 2012)

When terror tracers rend the night,
Sleeping birds in instant flight
Flee the darkness glowing bright.
Men in combat feeling fright.

Targets outlined on the screen,
Infrared shows moving green.
Men in motion flee the scene,
As bombs devour those unseen.

Mortars loud with bursting shell
Help create a living hell.
Bodies crisping where they fell
Phosphor burning and shrapnel.

Deafening quiet now we hear
No more laughter, no more tear.
Burnt to ashes, char, and sear.
Threat removed none left to fear.

Lived to fight another day.
Send them all to hell I pray.
Musn't tarry. Musn't stay.
Everything will be okay.

FIGHT OF THE PHOENIX

By Roy E. Peterson (November 20, 2012)
Tune of *Sink the Bismark*

I went to fight in Vietnam the country was a mess
And what we all were doing there was anybody's guess.
A communist insurgency was raging over there.
Our government said help our friend though war we won't declare.

I was a shirttail relative of the General Braxton Bragg,
Who fought for the Confederacy against the Union flag.
I had a warrior spirit inhabiting my soul.
I loved to fight for what was right when I was in control.

I learned that the insurgents were called the Viet Cong,
And when I learned their methods, I knew that they were wrong.
They simply killed the villagers and stole what they produced.
The Viet Cong were in the wrong and had to be reduced.

I trained as an advisor with a covert action program
To neutralize the Viet Cong and win in Vietnam.
I loved the special duty with the logo of the Phoenix.
Locate and assassinate with black op deadly tactics.

The program was invented by my friends at CIA
And given to the Army and to the green beret.
The ICEX then the Phoenix were sent to neutralize
Those who belong to Viet Cong and all that they comprise.

I wrote a book of my exploits the title is the same.
The *Fight of the Phoenix* the poem and book the name.
I helped to neutralize guerrilla Viet Cong.
In my time advising they lost four thousand strong.

I never fought a battle, but I fought a bloody war.
I designed the tactics in the Delta nothing more.
Coordinated actions and studied the intel.
I did my best to help the South and then I bid farewell.

PART II

MY SOCIETY

Waterfront Daydreams Painting
by Jane Scott Wooster

COAL EYES

By Roy E. Peterson (1965)

Coal Eyes, encased in a black limitless midnight of fur;
Glowing as though to say, "I have a hidden secret."
Indeed not one, but multitudinous they are;
Gleaned from my wanderings down alleys where people try
to forget.

I wander through those back streets little known to most
people
Where men are their basest selves and there's nothing to
prevent
The secret sins of the hidden slums, where enfeebled
Lie the morals of the heart in misery and contempt.

Little there is to be done for those wasters of life.
Life for them is something to escape from.
They shall find their escape, but their strife
Will not cease with death, when dark shadows come.

On some dark night they will inherit what they have sown—
A heritage trembling on sand and set in perilous places,
Where they shall be worth the worst they've ever know.
They shall disappear among that great sea of troubled faces.

I have seen what many souls are, yet I am not
A part of them, but rather, a shadowy ghost in the darkness
Pacing the streets wondering what inside they've lost
That leaves them in such a condition of loathsomeness.

I wonder in my own quiet way, as lightly I tread,
The reasons for their benighted downfall
What makes their lives so worthless and dead?
Why do they go on living at all?

Only existing because they have no hope or courage.
No courage to cease their useless activity,
Nor hope for a better tomorrow. They have been engaged
In a futile role as human beings of sanctity.

I move effortlessly, stealthily in their midst.
And they, unsuspecting, continue their self-desecration.
To their hidden slums I've paid many a visit
That revealed to me a most pitiful creation.

I walk in midnight and trace the failure of society.
Ever so incipiently I infiltrate and observe their lies.
I have seen portentous shadows of a doomed way
Of life. I tread only in darkness. I'm Coal Eyes.

I WATCHED A COUNTRY LOSE HER SOUL

By Roy E. Peterson (1967)

I watched a country lose her soul
A little at a time.
The first thing lost was reason,
The second thing was rhyme.

Perspectives on the common man
Men of strident zeal,
Once formed the sinews of this land,
They built her web of steel.

Once there was a Washington,
And once there was a Lincoln.
Once there was belief in God,
And once we were a beacon.

Music once came from the heart
From black and white alike.
It rolled across the grassy plains,
It pulled along the pikes.

"Erie Canal," "Sweet Betsy from Pike,"
"Clementine" and all
The songs of man that built this land
We seldom now recall

Lifestyles changed; perversions came;
We lost our will to win.
Our energy we self-consumed
And never found again.

The revolution wasn't war.
'Twas more the loss of soul.
It was a change in values
And partially of roles.

Freedom's bells are dormant now.
Dissent has hushed their tone.
Winds of change instead are heard
Like teeth of dog on bone.

It seems now Monkeys try to sing,
And Beetles rock and roll.
I watched a country lose her way,
Because she lost her soul.

OUR SELFISHNESS

By Roy E. Peterson (1970)

What a world of mercenaries we turned out to be.
Greedy, hungry people never caring if we're free;
Caring only for ourselves, and for the selfish ends we gain.
God must often ask Himself, "Did I create in vain?"

Every day we try to make ourselves what we are not.
Although we claim importance, we remain a little dot.
Alone, alone, always alone, we try to conquer all.
Yet, when we reach the top we find we still aren't quite so
tall.

Without the help of others we could never reach the top.
We're all in such a hurry we can never seem to stop.
We hurry, hurry, hurry, always hungering for more;
Always striving for new riches; never thinking 'bout the
poor.

Even in loves we try to get the most of it we can,
Never searching for the hidden truths; nor love the inner
man.
How selfishly we ply our trade and hurry on our way,
Never letting out our sunshine to cheer some soul each day.

BANK ROBBERS ROBBED US AGAIN

By Roy E. Peterson (November 20, 2012)

The bankers want our money to keep it safe for us.
Then banks will pay to others when you write out a check
I understand the nature of the banking business.
Banks can use your money for they have stacked the deck.

When we reached this decade of the twenty first century,
Bankers were in trouble for the homes loans they would do.
Banks again got greedy and dreamed up brand new fees.
To compensate for practices affecting me and you.

Bankers were forbidden from investing in a hedge.
By Act of Congress keeping safe deposits in their bank.
But then they passed a new law that took them to the edge.
Many bankers floundered and many bankers sank.

I remember years ago when bankers lost their shirt.
The Savings and Loan Scandal took us to recession
They started to go under and the little people hurt.
Congress had to step right in to keep us from depression.

This time between the hedge funds and making unsafe loans
The bankers played their poker games with funds that were not theirs.
If we had done what bankers did you'd hear a lot of groans.
For felonies committed in the name of earning shares.

It's hard to blame the bankers for holding out their hand
To the federal government and ask for billions more

For sins they had committed that helped them to expand,
While asking for forgiveness and all the rules ignore.

Congress was complicit in allowing home foreclosure
When banks had caused the problem by how they made a loan.
And Congress was persuaded of this I'm very sure
That they would reap the whirlwind from the seeds that they had sewn.

The banks again were robbers and stole our homes from us.
They started their foreclosures and called it due process.
They falsified the documents with signatures bogus
The crimes that they committed were sanctioned by our Congress.

The money that the big banks stole is monumental now.
The Congressmen assisted and joined the wrecking crew.
Instead of helping people with laws they did endow
The banks with all the money they stole from me and you.

I have learned a lesson. Commit the biggest crime.
They'll call it a new crisis, but not a felony.
They'll give you lots of money, but no one will do time.
And you will be rewarded by your own catastrophe.

The bankers are the robbers. They robbed us once again.
Foreclosures in the millions from crimes that they admitted.
And Congressmen should join them in the federal pen.
They all should be removed and they all should be committed.

They're planning their next robberies and never seem to stop

Free checking they'll get rid of and take more of our money.
We have to get new laws in place so we can call the cop
And we will be in reverie in the land of milk and honey.

We have to call our Congressmen and put up quite a fuss.
We have to sink the bankers 'cause the world depends on us.
Let's turn the fees around boys and then we'll have some fun
And shoot those robbing bankers and put them on the run.

BEWARE THE IVY BOUND TOWERS

By Roy E. Peterson (1969)

Beware the ivy bound towers of our academic society,
Where the vines of mistruth grasp at the mortar
Until brick after brick is loosened
Causing the foundation to crumble and fell the
superstructure.

Take note of the demise of the Athenian city state.
Debate, education, oratory, the Lyceum were all the rage.
Yet the glories of that well known polis
Are but intellectual ruminations from another age.

Stability is found where the boundaries of systems
Meet those of another and pass the test
Of time. Boundaries are porous membranes
To be maintained only by the power of self defense.

It is not the academic argument that maintains systems.
Nor is it an unprepared or foolish system that survives.
Rather it is the nation, state, society, man
That is sufficiently prepared who still thrives.

In the unmerciful light of historical research
May it be known by all lovers of freedom
That never has preparation been a virtue of democracy
And in today's world that spells doom.

TWINKIES FOREVER

Can be sung to the tune of *Jingle Bells*
By Roy E. Peterson (November 17, 2012)

A day or so ago,
I wanted a Ho Ho.
A Twinkie cake and Hostess pie
Were three things I could buy.
The grocer said no more,
For Hostess closed their store.
The Baker's Union went on strike.
They had to close the door.

Now what am I to do
For snack time after two
I want my Twinkies or a pie
Or Ho Hos till I die.
The Union is a flake
They took away my cake
I want to hunt them publicly
And burn them at the stake.

Chorus
Twinkie cakes, Twinkie cakes
They took you away.
I used to love to eat the goo
And Ding Dongs every day.
Twinkie cakes, Twinkie cakes
The Union caused your loss
How I'd like to find a way
To tar the Union boss.

PART III

MY HERITAGE

Harvesting Painting by Arnold Kramer 1912

AMERICAN HEARTLAND

By Roy E. Peterson (October 2, 2012)

The heartland of America,
Iron ore and river mica,
Starts just east of Ohio
Reaches Rockies capped with snow.

Canada to Texas plains
Nature's fields of golden grains;
Wheat and barley, corn and oats,
Ten thousand lakes with fishing boats.

Settlers came by wagon train
Summer heat or springtime rain.
Horse and buggy, Prairie Schooner
Oklahoma settled Sooner.

Bound together road and steel
Rubber tire, iron wheel.
Great Lakes, Rivers, freedom givers,
Bounty to the world delivers.

Bible teaching, Bible read,
Spirit filled, and Spirit led.
Go to church on Sunday morn.
Doesn't matter clothes outworn.

Know the value of a dollar
Education, future scholar,
Family time within the home,
Fertile soil of sandy loan.

Patriotic people they
Fly the flag Memorial Day.
Fireworks July the fourth
Match borealis in the North.

Silos in each Midwest town
Many boarded and shutdown.
Agribusiness now the rage,
Rulers of the purple sage.

Still the heartland proves its worth
Feed the nation; half the earth.
Hard work ethic, dinner pail
Tractor, wagon, hammer, nail.

Presidents keep their lookout
From their mountaintop redoubt.
Rushmore's craggy visages
Carved to last for all ages.

May they ever thus keep guard
Inspiring poet, patriot, bard.
May our country always stand
For values found in our heartland.

FARMER OF THE FORTIES

By Roy E. Peterson (October 24, 2012)

He fought the Second World War
And was one of the lucky men
Who wasn't shot, or maimed, or killed
And returned home safely again.
He could have worked in industry,
But preferred his fellow kinsmen.

At last reunited with family—
His wife and his two year old son.
Starting from scratch as a farmer,
But with skills and a double shotgun
A gift from the old generation
And work ethic second to none.

Powerful forearms and biceps
Built strong like a Grecian god
Blond head of a Nordic Viking
Blue sapphire eyes and square jawed
Legs like tree trunks standing
Shoulders expansive and broad.

At four in the early morning
He rises before first rays of sun
Come stealing over the prairie
He has chores that have to be done;
Milking the cows in the barnyard
Feeding the pig and the chicken.

Breakfast at eight in the morning,
Then out to the field to plow
The fresh smelling earth of the prairie
With free falling sweat on his brow.
His wife brings him lunch out at noontime
And he'll work long as light will allow.

Planting the fields in the springtime,
Alfalfa, oats, barley, wheat, corn.
Weeding the fields in the summer
Thistle, knapweed and rose thorn.
Harvesting grain in the autumn
In winter find calves newly born.

A Saturday bath is important
Before going to town for the night,
Walking the streets and just sitting
As friends stop and talk by streetlight.
Talk about farming and friendships
Gossiping, laughing outright.

Sunday he drives the eight miles
To church with his good family.
Reading the Bible and praying
The crops will produce mightily.
The cousins invited to dinner
Eat hearty and play happily.

His sister plays the piano.
Each kid must sing them a tune.
The relative audience clapping
As the music fills up the room.
His brother tells all some fun story
Before evening meal they consume.

The city folk think, "Oh how tedious"
The life of a farmer out there
Living somewhere on the prairie
The lives one could scarcely compare.
The farmer thinks, "Oh what a pity"
They can't smell the country night air.

Don't despair for the men of the prairie,
Or the comforts the country folk lack.
Early to bed just like Franklin
Advised in his old Almanac.
The breeze through the window is blowing
Perfume from the rose and lilac.

American heartland is beating
As hard working farmers still toil
In fields that are highly productive
Success re-enriching the soil;
Canning the fruit and the veggies;
And storing them so they can't spoil.

Farmers don't demand of their brother,
Or ask for a government check
As welfare just for their living,
Or damages just for the heck.
They don't ask for handouts or favors
They only ask just for respect.

Farmers are keepers of values
The city folk seem to forget.
The teacher of life that has meaning
A person that repays his debt.
Someone who still has a conscience;
Someone who has no regret.

The lessons I learned from my father
Have made me an honorable man.
I think of him living in heaven
Still doing the best that he can.
I thank him for being a beacon
And running the race that he ran.

SOUTH DAKOTA BOY

By Roy E. Peterson (September 24, 2012)

I come from South Dakota. In Winner I was born.
I've planted wheat and barley and shelled the golden corn.
I played in green alfalfa on browning stacks of hay.
I fed the pigs and chickens while doing chores each day.

I helped my dad with fences to corral the pigs and cows.
I got to drive the tractor and sharpen hoes and plows.
Sometimes I hoed the garden, sometimes the soy bean fields
To chop out all the weeds that grew and help increase the yields.

I've seen the roiling cloud mass as tornadoes swirled about.
"Get down into the cellar!" I heard my father shout.
The lightning strikes were brutal. The report would be so loud.
I thought that God was living in the blackened thundercloud.

The minute I saw green air the time had come to run,
For hailstones were coming, and they would spoil my fun.
The winds were fierce in winter as blizzards piled the snow.
A week was spent inside the house with just a radio.

I listened to the music that Lawrence Welk would play.
The Grain Belt Boys from Yankton would polka every day.
My father's favorite program was *Gunsmoke* Friday night,
And if I still could listen, *The Shadow* gave me fright.

Flash Gordon was my Sci-fi. *The Whistler* left me cold.
I loved *Big John and Sparky* and stories that they told.
I laughed at *Burns and Allen*, enjoyed the *Cisco Kid*,
I liked to hear Gene Autry sing and things Roy Rogers did.

Jack Benny and *Red Skelton*, the *Ozzie and Harriet* show,
Our Miss Brooks, Great Gildersleeve, and King Fish don't you know
Who appeared on *Amos 'n' Andy* were fun for everyone.
Mother liked *Ma Perkins, Drag Net*, and *Perry Mason*.

The shelter belt was planted in nineteen fifty-three.
A hundred trees were planted on the periphery
Protecting all the buildings, the grainary, barn, and house;
Along with all the animals and everything thereabouts.

The REA came to us in nineteen fifty-four.
But still we had no TV, since we were just too poor.
I was really thankful we had electric lights at last.
No more to fear the shadows the kerosene lantern cast.

My cousins were my best friends—Karen and Linda Lou,
Along with Riley and Nola. Oh what we five would do.
Every Sunday morning, we'd go to Sunday School.
Then church would come and pastor would teach the golden rule.

I remember harvest time the grain we'd stack in shocks.
Neighbors helped each other, then drive the grain to docks.
I helped unload the wagons at the elevator door
And then went back by tractor to help them load up more.

My mother paid a nickel for every fly I'd swat.
Sometimes I made a dollar and thought that was a lot.
The outhouse was two-seater, one hole large, one small.
A catalog for paper to wad into a ball.

We left the farm forever in nineteen fifty-six
And moved down to West Texas into a house of bricks.
My mother was a teacher and tripled our income.
A house with running water and paper for my bottom.

My mind turns back with fondness to the farm we left behind.
The work now seems so difficult, but then we didn't mind.
I never thought that I was poor. I had good food, a bed.
Our family loved each other. That's all that need be said.

LILACS AND ROSES

By Roy E. Peterson (November 26, 2012)

I never felt like I was poor while living on our farm.
A four room house was all we had with coal to keep us
warm.
I had one pair of blue jeans for making social calls
For school and for the farm chores I wore bib overalls.

I had to pump the water from a cistern to a pail.
I had to walk a quarter mile just to get the mail.
I had to slop the hogs and give the chickens feed.
Then milk the cows and toss them hay and plant the garden
seed.

The farm could smell to heaven and penetrate to hell.
When we ran out of water, we witched for a new well.
The outhouse built was sturdy and when we filled the pit,
My dad would put it on the skids and then we would move it.

Our barn was never painted like everybody should.
We couldn't spare the money to paint the weathered wood.
Dad joined with other farmers in a lumber sharing group.
When they tore the schoolhouse down, he built a chicken
coop.

At night we lit two lamps up that ran on kerosene.
You'd lift up the glass chimney and light the wick between.
Imagine doing homework by a flickering light.
We'd turn them off and go to bed in darkness every night.

Without electric power out there upon the prairie
I read the Holy Bible and then the dictionary.
If we wanted music, we'd bang on the piano.
No other entertainment, not even radio.

In autumn we would harvest and garden veggies can.
I thought it should be "jarring" I said with a deadpan.
The Mason jars were sealed up tight with lids and paraffin
And put down in our cellar to keep the food from rottin'.

Two things there were of beauty; two things of elegance.
The lilacs and the roses and their sweet fragrance
Were welcome blooms in springtime. They made quite a pair
As their blooming glory put perfume in the air.

Does it make a difference that my background I unsealed?
Does it make a difference that my past I have revealed?
The lesson that I'm teaching is there's beauty to be found
No matter where you come from, or where's your native ground.

BATTLE OF BONESTEEL

By Roy E. Peterson (September 25, 2012)

South Dakota joined the Union in eighteen eighty-nine.
The Rosebud Reservation was opened by design.
By eighteen ninety settlers had crossed the wide Missouri
Into eastern Gregory County, Dakota Territory.

Bonesteel was established in eighteen ninety two
With building of a store, saloon, and a casino crew.
A freighter gave a hundred if they named the town for him,
As money toward a schoolhouse including paint and trim.

When the railroad reached the outpost by nineteen zero two,
There was a plan for settlement as everybody knew.
Bonesteel was a tough town and by nineteen zero four
The gamblers and the outlaws made it rotten to the core.

Trains came pouring people in like an amazing race,
Thousands filed for homesteads and hoped to win a place.
One hundred sixty acres of land that they could win
Of just above 2,000 plots, the odds were pretty thin.

Chances on the lottery were one in forty-six.
The underworld saw Bonesteelers as pockets they could pick
And milk the gullible ones or simply steal their loot.
The Sheriff of the county sent out a call for troops.

The *New York Times* reported about the small ordeal
Suffered by the settlers and the Battle of Bonesteel.
They reported how the bad men had mugged the officers;
Took their guns and clubs first and then removed their stars.

The ones who won the lottery for land and settled down
Decided gamblers had to leave their thriving little town.
They rounded up the thieves and such by marching up new
Main

To take them to the jailhouse, or put them on the train.

The corps of solid citizens, two hundred by most counts,
Some with picks and shovels and others guns and mounts,
Stopped at every building and questioned occupants.
If they were not land owners, the charge was being vagrants.

Jim Gaughen was the judge and he was the jury too.
He openly presided over what became a zoo.
The townsmen had no patience. Immediately they pounced.
They ran the bad guys out of town before sentence was
pronounced

The settlers saved the town folk and killed a thug or two.
The slogan "Stand for no pinch" on the banner that they flew
Was repeated by the settlers as they quickly won the day.
The battle soon was over as the con men ran away.

PART IV

MY NATURE OBSERVATIONS

Photo: Lone Cypress on Monterrey Point titled
Sunset at Pebble Beach

NIGHT STORM

By Roy E. Peterson (1965)

Out of the dark came a strong wind.
Mystical were the elements as heaven began to rescind
The beauty of the previous day's creation
And extended an open invitation
To a dirge.

It seemed as though the fiends of Hell had been unleashed.
The devil himself had broken chains and released
His fury on the world; had loosed his anger
At being pent up; then had thrown his dagger
Of light

Again the wind changed, but now a cooling breeze
Blew gently through the trees.
Soft rain began to fall. Then I knew
My dreams had been invaded by a storm, which, too,
Refreshed nature.

NEW BIRTH

By Roy E. Peterson (1965)

Without a sea where would the rivers flow?
Their destiny no one would ever know.
Without a spring there'd be no love at all
To warm the heart.

When winter comes and hides away the sun,
Love's spring is gone and river's course is run'
Why grows the earth so cold and shadows fall?
Why comes the dark.

As man must do his best with sword or pen,
So life in spring must find new birth again.
The rivers wide must reach their sea and fall
Beneath the tide.

A BROOK'S WAY

By Roy E. Peterson (1970)

Old was the bridge and forlorn it looked.
Underneath trickled a small, lost brook.
It meandered here and wandered there,
While the bridge above much needed repair.

Stony was the path of the little lost brook.
I wondered why it, this course took.
In quest of an answer I walked its bed
Till I finally passed the bend ahead.

Then I knew why the brook had picked
This bed of stones and this path of sticks.
For around the bend the river it met.
It had chosen the quickest way it could get.

THE SEA

By Roy E. Peterson (1970)

The sea rolls on unchanged. Unmarred
By earthly wars it stays unscarred.
Always as long as man exists,
The sea will froth in perfect bliss.

When our life is borne away,
And fingers of sunlight point the way.
The sea will simply shrug it's shoal
For who shall stop its ebb and flow.

PARADISE FOUND

By Roy E. Peterson (1967)

Where's that wind leading me?
Somewhere I know.
Perhaps to the South Seas
Where soft trade winds blow.

A Paradise hidden, where we can stay
Away from the hustle of life everyday.
Way out on the azure blue sea there's a place
With fertile green valleys and mountains of lace.

LITTLE TRICK OF LAUGHING

By Roy E. Peterson (1966)

The little trick of laughing
When something goes astray
Is not to hide your head in shame
And look the other way.

Let in a little sunshine
And thank God for each day.
Then the little trick of laughing
Will roll the clouds away.

THE WORLD'S WITH YOU

By Roy E. Peterson (circa 1966)

Care and the whole world will care for you.
Share and the whole world will share with you.
Give and the whole world gives to you.
Live and the whole world comes alive.
Love and the whole world loves you.
Smile and the world is rosy too.
Play and the world becomes your playmate.
Pray and God will answer.
Seek and you will be found.

PANE OF ANOTHER DAY

By Roy E. Peterson (circa 1967)

The pane of another day
Invades the dream world
Wherein I lay
With my flag unfurled.

This, then, at last
Is the dawn. The bell
Rings for class.
Such bewilderment in a place I know so well!

Classtime and I
Must awake from sleep—
Somehow! A sigh . . .)
Is this the dawn for which I asked the night to retreat?

CLEAR IMAGE

By Roy E. Peterson (1964)

The sunlight danced and each ray glanced
Upon the mirror there.
And what it saw was not at all,
Because it didn't dare.

It didn't dare to be caught there
Alone with an image bright.
For if it were, its face would blur
And that did not seem right.

THE BEST COMES LAST

By Roy E. Peterson (1964)

The sun cannot shine till the clouds pass by.
Then comes the rainbow. I'll tell you why.
The fairest things are saved for the last my friend.
Things often are dark before light comes again.

The trialsome rain is a test, don't cry.
It waters the soil till the clouds roll by.
Then the sun comes out as if to say,
"I saved the best things for you today."

TAKE A STEP

By Roy E. Peterson (1964)

Sorrow's but an inch away from happiness.
Hate is but a step away from love.
The moon is but a stairway to the heavens.
It reflects the sunlight from above.

Just take a little moonbeam from the skyway.
Soon you'll find your dreams will all come true.
If you take a step, then grasp a sunbeam.
Happiness and love will come to you.

CONTRAST

By Roy E. Peterson (1963)

Two different poems by Shelley and Browning.
The latter one's bright and the former one's frowning.
A Dirge," and "Pippa Passes," how great is the contrast?
Would I wrote both, but my favorite's the last.

"All's right with the world," or "Wail for its wrongs."
Take your own pick of these two different songs.
But rather than wail for a world full of sorrow,
Think of new life and a better tomorrow.

A DAY OF GRACE

By Roy E. Peterson (1963)

Sometime the clouds will roll away.
Somewhere we'll find a better day.
And if this world gives no more grace,
Somewhere we'll know a better place.

Somehow when night takes over day,
And little sunbeams flit away,
I know who'll be in His place;
Ready to give of His free grace.

ONE SPRING DAY

By Roy E. Peterson (1964 & 2006)

Soft mist tickling fertile ground
The birds fell silent, not a sound.
That is until the sun came out
And then they all began to shout.

I gently picked the buttercup
And to the heavens I looked up
As birds began to get in tune,
The sun caressed the yellow bloom.

It seemed like all the flower beds
Were full of little sleepy heads.
The birds were singing "Get up now."
That's all the rest we can allow.

A bee came buzzing by my head.
I ducked about in perfect dread.
I saw the flowers welcome him,
And I deferred with just a grin.

It seemed as all the flowers in France
Had multiplied their fragrance.
The breeze caressed my lover's hair
As laughingly she caught me there.

PART V

MY FAMILY

American Gothic Painting by Grant Wood

TRIBUTE TO DAD

By Roy E. Peterson (1971 and 2006)

Meager were the fruits of labor
On the farm my dad once plowed.
But at night with toiling ended,
I could see him standing proud.

Proud of strength gleaned from each furrow,
As his muscles plied the sod.
Grateful for the help from heaven,
As his head he bowed to God.

He is smiling down on us now.
He has made his last homerun.
Heaven's gates were opened quickly,
For they knew what he had done.

Always faithful to his duties,
He is resting now in peace.
He is in his home in heaven
Where his soul has found release.

Those who've gone before give comfort.
"Welcome, son, what took so long?"
Mother, father, sister, brother
All the friends who joined the throng.

Oh, I know he's waiting for us
Right beside the shining sea.
All around is heaven's glory
As he waits for you and me.

ELEGY FOR MOM

By Roy E. Peterson (2009)

My mom was small, but was not frail.
She took the tiger by the tail.
Mom was fearless, brave, and true
She praised the Lord in all she'd do.

The banking crash of '27
Happened when she was eleven.
Her grandpa lost the bank and then
Repaid the customers, every one.

In that same year she lay in bed
With polio from toes to head.
She loved to climb up in the trees,
Till polio brought her to her knees.

The Great Depression left her poor,
And was reflected in what she wore.
Mom made her dresses from flour sacks
And rarely went to store bought racks.

Her father often taught the family lessons
And took a job at Dakota Wesleyan
To make sure his four children had a way
To go to college everyday.

Mom's mother studied oratory
At a Chicago conservatory.
Mom's father maximized his talent.
Accountant, teacher, superintendant.

They all were raised up Methodist,
Till dancing made them all Baptist.
When Methodists accepted dance,
They left the church in defiance.

Mom was a Dakota resident
And was elected President
Of Baptist Youth throughout the state
Where she met dad, 'twas more than fate.

Mom was a singer, painter, teacher,
And a Temperance Union speaker.
Mom was shy, but quite a leader
When every organization needed her.

Mom did not have a life of ease,
But always taught me to say please.
She taught me when the day was gone
To thank the Lord for what he'd done.

Her favorite flower was the lily,
And loved it when I acted silly.
Her tastes were simple, pleasures few;
Like mornings with a heavy dew.

I never heard her laugh so hard,
As when I ran back in the yard.
I jumped around like I was drunk
And yelled at Mom, I met a skunk.

Mom loved collecting recipes
I loved her Dusty Miller cookies.
While garden planting in the spring
I soon would hear her start to sing.

The thing that I remember most
Was that she never liked to boast.
She had a world class solo voice
That must have made the heav'ns rejoice.

I think that I can hear her now
"I'd Rather Have Jesus Anyhow."
Her voice is lilting, soaring higher
While singing in the Angel Choir.

GRANDFATHER OF THE MIDDLE PRAIRIE

By Roy E. Peterson (November 25, 2012)

He was born to pioneers, Dakota Territory.
Lived on a homestead not far from Purgatory.
They staked a claim near Geddes, it was a farming town.
Great Grandpa said its far enough it's time to settle down.

Great Grandpa Backus was a judge for he had studied law.
They said he was the fairest that anybody saw.
His sons all worked the homestead from morning till sundown
While he took care of business in the little local town.

My grandpa had three brothers and a sister they named Nell.
John and Ben and Reno the stories they could tell,
Like how a prairie fire approached their little farm,
But then the wind had shifted and they were saved from harm.

John became the Agent of the Greenwood Agency
In charge of all the Indians and of their families.
When Indians started drinking and landed in the jail,
His duty was to get them out and help them make their bail.

Uncle Ben had fought in France in the First World War.
He suffered from some mustard gas and wounds that he bore.
But he was quite a salesman and managed local stores.
His lungs for life affected and he could not work outdoors.

Nellie soon got married and went to California.
Her husband planted orange tree groves near sunny Santa Paula.
I remember every Christmas we really got a lift
They sent a crate of oranges for our Christmas gift.

Reno was the youngest and did not like the prairie.
First he became a doctor and then a missionary.
As soon as he got married, they went to Carolina
To prepare for missions and then they went to China.

Grandpa Backus studied law at Dakota Wesleyan.
Francis Case was in his class, but grandpa was best man.
Francis Case became a lawyer; then a Senator.
One day I got to meet him, when he came through the door.

Next Grandpa took accounting and again was number one.
He had a double major when his student days were done.
He headed for Chicago, for the University,
Where he could take accounting and political economy.

While there he met a lady at the Conservatory,
Who studied declamation, debate, and oratory.
The daughter of a banker in Carroll, Iowa,
She was used to finer things than was my good grandpa.

Soon after they were married they headed for Smithwick,
The county of Fall River, where they could take their pick
Of homesteading locations by my grandpa and his bride.
They put their stakes into the ground. The claims were side
by side.

Two buckboards and four horses they drove the wagon trail
Through springtime rains and thunderstorms and even
through the hail.
They came upon some Indians still living in their tepee.
The Indian brave said you are at the place called Wounded
Knee.

Where once there was a battle, the wagon trail split.
The Indian brave said take the left, you quickly must
commit.
An old man with a tomahawk came charging from the tent
They swiftly took the left fork and down the trail they went.

When they approached the Badlands on their way to the Black Hills,
They stopped nearby a farmstead with water from windmills.
He told the story to me as I saw a Badlands mug
And we were sitting in the place that now was called Wall Drug.

They spent a year near Smithwick in order to prove claim.
Each one could then get registered if they used their own name.
They built a shack that straddled their adjacent claiming line.
When they had spent a year there, the land they could combine.

My Grandpa and my grandma had a four kid family.
Two were boys and two were girls, intelligent and friendly.
I still don't know what happened as my grandma moved away
And wound up in Muskogee, Oklahoma where she stayed.

Grandpa was a teacher in Grand Rapids, Michigan.
The brothers of my grandma tried to put him into prison.
They garnisheed his wages when they filed a legal claim.
Grandpa won his case in court, but sullied his good name.

At first he worked the oilfields they found in Wyoming.
The Coburn brothers tracked him, so he had to keep on moving.
He headed then for Spokane in the state of Washington.
Became a migrant worker picking strawberries in the sun.

My grandma sold her daughters to a newly wealthy lady.
Grandpa learned what happened and he knew the deal was shady.
My mom was only four years old and her sister only two.
Grandpa found the lady and told her he would sue.

He found out that the brothers of my grandma got the fee.
My grandpa paid a ransom just to set the sisters free.
The boys they stayed with grandma and the girls with grandpa.
The boys grew up in Tulsa and the girls in Dakota.

Again he started teaching; then came the Great Depression.
He taught and was accountant at Dakota Wesleyan.
My grandma died in Tulsa from a fire that she set.
The boys were fine, but were unwanted after that.

The brothers and the sisters were united once again.
My grandpa found what happened and he took the boys right in.
Because he was accountant and teacher it was free
For his kids to graduate from the university.

The Second World War came next and he was over fifty.
Too old to fight in battle, but he thought he had a duty.
He sent an application to the brand new Pentagon
The Navy hired grandpa as accountant thereupon.

He moved into a boarding house in Washington, DC
He joined in the war effort to keep our liberty.
He criticized the practices at his accounting station.
He argued with his Navy boss and gave his resignation.

He bought a house in Omaha and went to work at Boeing.
His work there was respected and reports of him were glowing.
While dad was in the Army, my mother moved me there.
I was only one year old and wasn't much aware.

When the war was over Boeing cut the work force quota.
Then he returned to teaching in a town in South Dakota.
At first it was in Wheeler and then in Bonesteel.
He kept right on a teaching when the made him Principal.

On weekends he would pick me up and we'd hunt rocks and
arrows.
He taught me every bird name from the robins to the
sparrows.
His lapidary hobby was making jewelry
From agates that we found and polished till they're pretty.

He made me read the Bible and took me to the choir.
He taught me about Jesus and of the hellish fire.
Besides the *Bobbsey Twin* Books he gave me for my birthday,
I had to read *The Fall of Rome* and use the dictionary.

In summer when not teaching he would head for the Black
Hills,
Where he had built a wooden shack with very little frills.
He called it Custer Rock Shop; his jewelry displayed;
Besides the souvenirs there, he sold what he had made.

I could end this epic with the day that Grandpa died,
But that would be too simple because I take my pride
In all the stories told me and lots of things I do.
Like polishing the agates and making homemade stew.

The greatness of a grandpa is wisdom that he gives
To his next generations as if his spirit lives.
My grandpa was a Grandfather of the Middle Prairie.
I know he is in heaven now in that great lapidary.

PART VI

MY MUSIC

Music Digital Photo Manipulation

BLACKBERRY PICKING MORNING, MINNESOTA KIND-OF-A-DAY

By Roy E. Peterson (Copyright 1974 and 2006)

(Chorus) It's a blackberry picking morning, it's a Minnesota
kind-of-a-day.
All the corn is growing and the breeze is blowing,
everything's going to by okay.
All the springtime flowers are blooming. All my cares have
gone away.
It's a blackberry picking morning, it's a Minnesota
kind-of-a-day.

There's a white frame house 'neath a band of trees, there's a
peacefully flowing stream,
That I followed away, when I left one day to find the
American dream.
There's a barefoot boy who grew to a man, who is longing to
hear someone say,
It's a blackberry picking morning, it's a Minnesota
kind-of-a-day.

It's a blackberry picking morning, it's a Minnesota
kind-of-a-day.
All the corn is growing and the breeze is blowing,
everything's going to by okay.
All the springtime flowers are blooming. All my cares have
gone away.
It's a blackberry picking morning, it's a Minnesota
kind-of-a-day.

It's the Land of Lakes that are calling me, and the woods I
used to roam.
In the wintertime, it's the logs of pine that are burning on
my mind.
There are summer showers and happy hours. There is some
sweet girl to say,

"It's a blackberry picking morning, it's a Minnesota
kind-of-a-day."

It's a blackberry picking morning, it's a Minnesota
kind-of-a-day.
All the corn is growing and the breeze is blowing,
everything's going to by okay.
All the springtime flowers are blooming. All my cares have
gone away.

It's a blackberry picking morning, it's a Minnesota
kind-of-a-day.

TUCSON SUNDAY MORNING

By Roy E. Peterson (Copyright 1974 and 2006)

(Chorus) Tucson Sunday morning, see the sage brush come alive.
Gold upon the Rincons, Catalina mountain sides.
Saguaro in the desert lift their silent arms in prayer.
The mission bell is tolling, my stage will soon be rolling,
But my dreams will still be there.

Cantina of Alinda, where I bedded for awhile.
Was it the fiery liquor, or the senorita's smile.
Warm nights with soft Alinda. Palo Verde scented hair.
When I awoke it was the dawn and I had to travel on,
But my dreams will still be there. (Chorus Repeat)

They found another Marshall. Said he's riding in today.
It's time that I was leaving for the border anyway.
The vision of Alinda with a flower in her hand
Will bring me back some midnight when the moon is shining bright
On the Tucson golden sand. (Chorus Repeat)

Gunfighter's life is anguish, always danger in the air.
I headed for Alinda, though I knew I shouldn't dare.
Tucson streets were empty; caught a flash of forty-four.
Is that really you Alinda? Am I at your hacienda?
Is that my body lying there? (Chorus Repeat)

ALL MY TOMORROWS: WEDDING SONG

By Roy E. Peterson (January 2011)

1

From this day forward, forever my love
I pledge to you darling and God above.
I'll never forsake you and always will be
Right here to protect you and keep you by me.

Chorus

All my tomorrows I give to you
All of my heartbeats, forever true
Each breath I take; each step of my life
You're walking there with me as man and wife.

2

Forsaking all others I give all my wealth
For richer or poorer, in sickness in health
I'll cling to you always as long as I live
With this ring I wed thee and all my love give.

Chorus

All my tomorrows I give to you
All of my heartbeats, forever true
Each breath I take; each step of my life
You're walking there with me as man and wife.

3

Though death will come dear and take one away
I'll watch you from heaven by night and by day.
Then we'll be together my darling once more
As we walk together on heaven's bright shore.

Chorus

All my tomorrows I give to you
All of my heartbeats, forever true
Each breath I take; each step of my life
You're walking there with me as man and wife.

LOST MINER

By Roy E. Peterson (1961 and 2006)

The desert tells the story of the past so long ago
Of a trusting miner and his faithless partner, Joe.
He left his wife and children looking for the mother lode.
They struck it rich in Prescott, had their cabin filled with
gold.

His partner almost killed him, left him on the ground for
dead.
Somehow he stayed alive with one bullet to the head.
The miner kept on searching for another golden mine,
But instead he found that drinking occupied his precious
time.

By his greed and the devil, he kept up his search.
Till one day he stopped by an old country church.
There for a while he remembered his love fair,
But the greed and the devil wouldn't leave him there.

It was in the Superstitions that the Dutchman made his find.
Ever since a load of people have been searching for his mine.
We may never know what happened to the Dutchman and
his gold,
For he disappeared from history, though his tale has long
been told.

Some say he left for Frisco, some say he left for France.
Some say they thought they saw him do a devil of a dance.
As for me I have a feeling that he headed for the coast.
And the searchers for his gold mine have been looking for
his ghost.

I MAY NEVER PASS THIS WAY AGAIN

By Roy E. Peterson (1979 and 2006)

I may never pass this way again.
Believe in Jesus as your savior, my friend.
When shadows move across the land,
He will take you by the hand,
For I may never pass this way again.

All my life I longed for someone to care.
My burden heavy and there's no one to share.
Then the Master's hand I found,
And my fetters he unbound.
Now I will never pass that way again.

I may never pass this way again.
Believe in Jesus as your savior, my friend.
When shadows move across the land,
He will take you by the hand,
For I may never pass this way again.

Well my friend, he sent me by your way.
Now you're waiting at life's crossroads today.
You must decide which way to go.
You must answer, "Yes, or No."
To the savior as I hear him say:

I may never pass this way again.
Believe in Jesus as your savior, my friend.
When shadows move across the land,
I will take you by the hand,
For I may never pass this way again.

I'LL MEET YOU TOMORROW

By Roy E. Peterson (December 2006)

I'll meet you tomorrow, for I know you'll have a new place.
Gonna miss you so.
Know you had to go,
But someday I'll look on your face.
Don't worry 'bout leaving. For the path is clear up ahead.
They are calling you.
You will make it through
The long valley of death we all dread.

[Refrain] My eye's on the sparrow and you know how I care
for you.
Feel the golden sound
Love is all around
Let my light come shining through.
I have prepared the table of mercy and goodness.
I will give you rest
You have passed the test.
You have proved to me your worthiness.

I'll meet you tomorrow, for I'll hear your voice way out
there.
Singing out to me
Like it used to be.
As you rocked me to sleep in the chair.
My soul will be lifted as I see your face from afar.
Softly smiling down
Sunshine all around
Singing lead in heaven's grand choir.

I'll meet you tomorrow, kinfolk crowding all around
Some I never knew
Will be there with you
How I'm glad that I have been found
I'll see you in heaven and I'll hear the music again
That is still for now
As my head I bow.
But I keep on hearing that refrain.

BECKY WAS A TWIRLER

By Roy E. Peterson (1961)

Becky was a twirler, practiced day and night.
Everything she did, it always turned out right.
Figure trim and slender;
Lips so warm and tender;
Oh how she smiled when she marched in line.
Closely I would watch her.
You never saw a twirler
Like my little Becky keeping time.

I was proud of her when she walked down the field,
But I kept the feelings of my heart concealed.
I watched from the stands
As Becky led the band;
And I smiled at her in the majorette line.
She was very pretty,
It's really quite a pity,
That we didn't share a lot of time.

Faster and faster, she whirled ever faster.
There was no one else could twirl like her.
Round and round so fast,
I wished our kiss would last.
She had turned my heart upside down.
Walked her off the field
Oh how her eyes revealed
A sweetness that would twirl me all around.

Kisses that we shared, showed how much we cared
For each other as we dared.
Hearts were twirling fast,
I wanted them to last,
But I knew that soon I had to go away.
When I left for college,
To get a lot more knowledge,
Then our kisses ended on that day.

LAST DATE (Tune of Last Date)

By Roy E. Peterson (1961)

This shall be our last date.
That's the decree of fate.
For the last time we shall kiss.
Then depart, Tears will start, Tear each heart, all apart.
This shall be my last kiss on your lips.

Time has stepped in between.
Our breakup was foreseen.
Last night you were out late
With someone, now it's done, he has won, must be fun.
Now I know this shall be our last date.

One kiss then I shall go.
To where I do not know.
I used to love you so.
But I see, there will be someone else meant for me.
I shall kiss this last kiss, then I'll go.

PRETTY LITTLE TEXAS GIRLS (Music)

By Roy E. Peterson (1976)

Pretty little Texas girls; Oh pretty little Texas girls.
Eyes are bright; teeth are pearls, soft hair falling down in
curls!
Pretty little Texas girls; Oh pretty little Texas girls.
In Texas towns they're all around. Those pretty little Texas
girls.

Down in San Anton, you're never left alone.
In Angelo or El Paso—No matter where you go
Those Texas girls that I love so
Will swing you to and fro.
It'll break your heart to be apart from pretty little Texas girls.

Pretty little Texas girls; Oh pretty little Texas girls.
Eyes are bright; teeth are pearls, soft hair falling down in
curls!
Pretty little Texas girls; Oh pretty little Texas girls.
In Texas towns they're all around. Those pretty little Texas
girls.

In Lubbock, Fort Worth, Austin—Abilene I know
Ya'll are there. You know I care. It's almost more than I can
bear
To leave you for awhile, so give me one more smile.
It will break my heart to be apart from pretty little Texas
girls.

Pretty little Texas girls; Oh pretty little Texas girls.
Eyes are bright; teeth are pearls, soft hair falling down in
curls!
Pretty little Texas girls; Oh pretty little Texas girls.
In Texas towns they're all around. Those pretty little Texas
girls.

I love Cowgirls in Dallas, and Kilgore Rangerettes.
There are Tyler roses in sexy poses that I cannot forget.
So if you hear my song, you know it won't be long
Until I find my state of mind with pretty little Texas girls.

Pretty little Texas girls; Oh pretty little Texas girls.
Eyes are bright; teeth are pearls, soft hair falling down in curls!
Pretty little Texas girls; Oh pretty little Texas girls.
In Texas towns they're all around. Those pretty little Texas girls.

PART VII

MY HISTORY AND LEGENDS

Paul Bunyan Watercolor

THE LEGEND OF TEXAS TROOPER SAMMY LONG

A True Poetic Story
By Roy E. Peterson (February 2012)

Whenever West Texas tales are told,
Some speak of oil or Maximilian's gold,
Some of Judge Bean and his Pecos law,
And some of John Wesley Hardin's draw.

But I tell the legend of Sammy Long
A highway patrolman big and strong.
Who lived in McCamey, a West Texas town
And married the HomeEc teacher, Miss Brown.

The kids all thought they were getting away
With races by night and tricks by day.
For some reason it never occurred to us,
Sammy would talk to our parents and discuss—

What they should do and please don't tell
That Sammy knew our deeds and us very well.
The kids didn't know how the parents found out
What they were doing and what they were about.

Sammy protected the kids from shame,
But everyone knew who they should blame
For whatever happened and he would know
Who did what to whom at the drive-in show.

You better not speed or drive while drunk
Or you might end up in Sammy's trunk.
As kids we had a healthy fear
Of Sammy, but yet we felt secure.

A California stranger one fateful day
Was stopped by Sammy on the Rankin highway.
Sammy didn't know that he was on the run,
But the stranger opened fire with a .32 gun.

A shot hit Sammy and brought him down.
The stranger shot six times in his back on the ground.
A deer hunter saw what was going on
And that a stranger shot Sammy Long.

The man was returning from a hunting trip.
He took out his rifle and he fired a clip.
The report said the hunter shot the stranger dead
With lots of bullets. He was full of lead.

All in McCamey mourned the friend they had
With tears from every mom and kid and dad.
I like to think Sammy still rides erect
On the roads of West Texas to serve and protect.

THE TRAPEZE ARTIST WHO NEVER LEFT

DEDICATED TO THE MEMORY OF PANSY
(FANNIE CARPENTER)
By Roy E. Peterson (April 1, 2012)

The first time that I saw her I asked who could she be.
A shambling dirty woman you never hope to see.
Her hair was long and scraggly. Her dress was long and
torn.
I wondered when I saw her, who could look so all forlorn.

She was pulling a dark red wagon, a Radio Flyer toy,
Along an unpaved alley, while staring at some boy.
I saw her then stoop over and pick up a tin can.
The boy got out of there quickly as far away he ran.

I followed at a distance; I had never seen such sight
In this West Texas setting, it just did not seem right.
She found a piece of junk there and figured it was good
And as she shuffled along, she checked the bins for food.

I learned they called her Pansy, but never found out why
Her name was changed from Fannie. I didn't want to pry.
Her house was old scrap lumber; a shack in an oil town,
Where both she and the town folk had better days there
known.

The kids all called her crazy. The boys would tease and run.
The rumors were that Pansy could really shoot a gun.
My parents new to Texas in the '50's talked to her,
While I sat in the back seat of the car a listener.

My parents asked what they could do to help her in her need.
She said she needed nothing, but thank you for the deed.
Although her voice was gruff like, she had a softer side.
That changed my mind about her. I'm sure she had her pride.

She was a living legend, depends how old you are.
She arrived there in McCamey in a Ford A model car.
Her named was Fannie Carpenter and yes it was a fact.
Her husband made the duo for their high wire act.

The oil came in gushers and there was so much crude
10,000 quickly rushed there, the strong, the brave, the shrewd.
They needed entertainment, so a circus with its duo
Displayed the Flying Carpenters who put on quite a show.

Sweet Pansy was a beauty, long curls cascading down
Her golden tresses blowing as they drove first into town.
With shoulders bare through windows, she was like a movie star.
The men would look with longing as she travelled in the car.

In 1926 McCamey, they flew on their trapeze
And walked the tight rope lightly and did their act with ease.
But one night something happened to the two so well renowned.
Without a safety net they fell; their bodies hit the ground.

Her husband tried to save her and as they hit the earth,
He cradled her above him and kept her from sure death.
But Pansy hit her head hard, her head was injured bad.
Her husband died most instantly some think it drove her mad.

She never left McCamey as every day she'd grieve.
She felt her soul was stuck there, his grave she couldn't leave.
Though hundreds tried to court her, she never let them stay
Politely she would thank them and send them on their way.

She could have lived with family in Medina County where
She grew up, attended school, but she would not go there.
A recycler before the word came into the lexicon,
She built her own small house there with lumber she had sawn.

She was self sufficient, although she was petite.
She built on a garage there and set the Ford in concrete.
A monument to her husband, who had saved her life that night,
She never learned to drive it, but kept it out of sight.

She could not make a living back with the circus tent.
So she built little houses for oilfield workers rent.
They say that she put wood doors upon discarded cars
And rented them to desperate men who had to sleep in bars.

There was a dearth of housing in those early years out there
Where fire ants and rattlers were more than one could bear.
Pansy sewed the curtains and there are testaments
She added on the porches and turned tin to ornaments.

Her beauty sadly faded, her renters came and went
Just like the dream attraction had left the circus tent.
She became a scavenger for bottles and for tin,
For boards and metal roofing, and looked in every bin.

They say that every now and then when her funds were low
She'd walk the 94 miles to the town San Angelo,
Where she would do her banking and could be seen beside
The highway there a walking and never take a ride.

The few who went to see her said on her behalf
She looked like Mary Pickford in an aging photograph
That sat on a piano a memento of her past.
A reminder of her beauty and things that cannot last.

Though children were afraid there was no cause for alarm.
It was only her appearance. She never meant them harm.
She often shared with others the things that she would find
The one's she thought were worse off—The deaf, the dumb, the blind.

In failing health no longer could Pansy live alone.
She sold the Model A then, the only car she'd owned.
She left her life of sorrow and living second rate
And died in Kerrville hospital at the age of 78.

The town remembers Pansy, an eccentric character.
But I have seen the vision of the beauty that was her.
Within my heart are images I wish I could dispel
And hope she went to heaven, since living was her hell.

HOW MAXIMILIAN LOST HIS TREASURE

By Roy E. Peterson (April 2012)

The only Imperial Treasury lost in the American West
Purportedly was never found, but many have been obsessed.
The Civil War was raging and while restoring order,
The US with its trouble could not look beyond its border.

Meanwhile in France Napoleon the third had won election,
And abolished the Republic and with a single action,
Declared himself the Emperor of the Second Empire there,
But an Emperor without Empire was more than he could bear.

The nephew of Napoleon did something quite absurd
As France allied with Mexico, another Empire he declared.
While America was diverted and focused on its war,
Napoleon seized control there in 1864.

He selected for sub-Emperor the Archduke Ferdinand
To go there with Carlota and control the foreign land.
So Ferdinand Maximilian moved to Mexico
And called himself the Emperor with his inflated ego.

To be a Duke in Austria was really common fare,
But add the title, Emperor, and you had something rare.
He seized on opportunity that fell into his lap.
It's said that neither one could find the Empire on a map.

The move was but good politics with Max's brother Franz
The Emperor of Austria to help align with France.
The excuse for taking over was default on the debts
That Mexico owed foreign banks and had no more assets.

At first the wealthy landowners were ones supporting Max,
But liberal reforms of Juarez, he just would not rollback.
The Republicans of Juarez who had lost their government
Hated that an Austrian with French troops had been sent.

The Civil War had ended and by 1866,
Attention turned to Mexico and Latin Republics.
America told Napoleon, get French troops out of there
And take out Maximilian or else they best beware.

Now Max who was no dummy decided to retire
To his castle back in Austria and get out of the fire,
But to be a proper gentleman he needed to be rich.
A mountain of gold and silver he thought would do the
trick.

It could not go to Veracruz. It would arouse suspicion.
He had to send it secretly with a military mission.
The cover used was bags of flour and barrels for disguise
And tell the wagon masters to hide from prying eyes.

The treasure passed Presidio on its way to Galveston,
Where ships were waiting patiently to take the treasure on.
The Rio Grande was passable at that time of year.
They headed into Texas, a Wild West frontier.

The fifteen wagon convoy was guarded by just four
Austrian soldiers riding. They should have sent some more.
Soon after reaching Texas somewhere across the Rio,
They met Confederate soldiers escaping to Mexico.

The men were from Missouri and told what lay between
The wagon train and San Antone and all that they had seen.
As they were riding southward they met some bandit gangs
And six reported Indians a riding on mustangs.

The Austrians hired the Missourians for protection of the
"flour".
The Missourians got curious and wondered at their ardor.
No doubt it seemed quite strange to them that "flour" had
an escort,
Especially of Austrians of the military sort.

One night near Horse Head Crossing along the Pecos bank
Five Missourians lured the guards away, the sixth came from
the flank.
He moved between the wagons with his metal tools
He pried the barrels open and saw the gold and jewels.

When he reported what he'd seen to the conspirator
They decided that the Austrians they soon would
overpower.
They made a pact to share the loot and then they made a
plan
That they would strike the next day and take all that they
can.

Six wagons they could manage with all the teamsters dead
And all the Austrians shot to death some miles from Horse
Head.
The following night the caravan was camped at Castle Gap
A cut between the mesas. A place marked on their map.

Two Austrian were sleeping, while two were standing guard.
The fifteen Mexican teamsters were sleeping pretty hard.
Four shots rang out and killed the guards before they knew
what hit.
And then the fifteen teamsters took the second hit.

Nineteen men were slaughtered. No one was left to fight
And then the band of soldiers decided there that night
They could not move the wagons and outride on the side.
A bad idea to kill the teamsters with fifteen tons to hide.

They moved the treasure nearby and released the oxen
teams.
Then they hid the treasure, the stuff that's made of dreams.
It took a while to dig the pit and bury all the loot
An entire Imperial treasury and 19 dead men mute.

Each man had packed his horses with all the coin they'd
carry
And headed out for San Antone for Indians being wary.
When two days they had ridden one of the men got ill
He dropped out for a rest. It's said they shot him on a hill.

There was no trust among them, they figured he'd return
To the buried loot and take it from the place the wagon's
burned
To mark the treasure hidden beneath the sandy soil
In some forsaken canyon beneath the charred topsoil.

They continued on without him assuming he was dead,
But the wounded man recovered from the bullets made of
lead.
He headed toward San Angelo, the first fort on the way
Along the trail to San Antone by night and not by day.

He struggled cross West Texas along the trail and then
He came upon the bodies of the five Missouri men.
Their saddle bags were empty and scattered all around
Perhaps Comanche raiders had left them on the ground.

He was the last survivor of a total twenty-five
Who had started on the journey and he was scarce alive.
He kept on struggling forward and one evening saw a fire
A camp set up by horse thieves; his circumstance dire.

He bedded down as night fell, but just before the dawn
A sheriff's posse caught them and took them into town.
The sheriff he just figured that he was one of them,
And threw him in the jail cell among the other men.

It took him some convincing to get him out of jail,
By then a strong infection helped him get his bail.
They took him to a doctor and just before he died
He told the doc this story and swore 'twas not a lie.

He related this whole story and then he drew a map.
X marks Horse Head Crossing and X marks Castle Gap.
Years went by before the doc and his attorney traveled out
To dig for buried treasure. No Comanche left about.

The Indian wars subsided and on the frontier land
The Army did its job well and held the upper hand.
They could not find the landmarks though they left no stone
unturned
And they could find no evidence of the wagon train they'd
burned.

They say no one has found it, an entire treasury.
Perhaps the place where it lies buried no one will ever see.
For those that are still searching, I offer this advice
If one can ever view the map try folding it up twice.

Another theory have I about the hidden hoard,
Some markers are extinguished and have to be ignored.
The sandstorms of West Texas will quickly change the face
Of anything that's standing in that arid place.

Ten miles north of McCamey if you will drive or fly a plane
You look off to the right of the highway going toward Crane.
You will not need a compass, nor a highway map
You'll see as big as Texas the place named Castle Gap.

I've been there twice while hiking. The rancher gave
permission
For me to make the journey on a Sunday morn excursion.
Some men have brought in dozers, and others a back hoe
To dig for buried treasure, but never found a peso.

This story's more than legend. This story's based on fact.
The Treasury was missing, when Benito's men came back.
The doctor and attorney in this story were quite sure
The man who told the story was dying with no cure.

BILLY SOL AND THE FERTILIZER TANKS

By Roy E. Peterson (March 30 2012)

A good ol' boy from Pecos, name of Billy Sol
Did something quite outrageous and hid it from the law.
A governmental program could pay the rent on tanks
Containing fertilizer so Billy said, "Why Thanks!"

Billy Sol was partnered with a man called LBJ,
Who in turn was VP under President JFK.
A key campaign contributor to the Democratic cause
Billy Sol was confident that he could skirt the laws.

Billy Sol claimed mortgages on tanks out in the field
Where anhydrous ammonia within the tanks were sealed.
He used the fraudulent mortgage scheme to obtain loans
from banks
Using as collateral nonexistent fertilizer tanks.

He told one of his partners and said it with some mirth,
"I think the Ag inspectors, are stuck there in Fort Worth."
The good ol' boys got richer with profit from the deal.
The Democrats were paid off and none of them would
squeal.

Billy Sol got greedy and planned another scheme.
Although it was illegal, it worked just like a dream.
He purchased large allotments of cotton based on land
That farmers would first purchase from Billy Sol's own
hand.

Then he would lease the land back and allotments from the
farm
He told the local farmers his scheme would do no harm.
After one year, was the first date to make payment, but who
knew
That Billy Sol had told them to default when mortgages were
due.

The plan went on unhindered; for several years it ran.
The cotton allotment transfers made him a wealthy man.
Though it was quite illegal these Billy Sol antics
He dismissed the allegations as just being politics.

One day his schemes collapsed. The judge said fraud's the
reason.
Your cotton and your fertilizer are taking you to prison.
Out there in Pecos, Texas they call it Estes Sunday
When people hunt for fertilizer. Forget the Easter Bunny.

MY TEXAS HOMETOWN CONFESSIONS

By Roy E. Peterson (March 2012)

I claim a Texas hometown not where born, but raised.
I moved there as a teenager back in my halcyon days.
Coming from a Northern state I had a little shock
Because my new surroundings were made of caliche rock.

That was not the only thing to take me by surprise.
There were a lot of changes I had to realize.
In class I had to answer teacher with the phrase "Yes,
ma'am".
And "lickings" made me eager to get with the program.

For those who are not Texan and don't know what I mean
A licking with a paddle made every school kid scream.
It helps you pay attention to what the teacher says
And never ask a neighbor if they would pass the "Pez".

If I had a quarter, I'd run to Mr. Mack's,
Where I would order Frito Pie and other Texas snacks.
A Moon Pie made of chocolate or pecan pie would do.
RC or Dr. Pepper to drink when I was through.

The eighth grade was my entry upon the Texas scene.
Puberty had hit me hard as I had turned thirteen.
The Southern drawl of Texan girls drove me up the wall.
I wanted to be with them, and loved them one and all.

A girl I fell in love with let me touch her inner thigh
The eighth grade desks were doubles and hid the things I'd
try.
The music played was Elvis and Buddy's "Peggy Sue."
The girls wore crinoline hoop skirts, the meat was barbeque

My fantasies were heightened when I had my first real kiss.
I thought that I found heaven and dreamed in perfect bliss.
Parties there were monitored, but we played "Kiss, Go Walk,
or Slap"
And sometimes in my homeroom a girl sat on my lap.

My high school days were special, now that I look back.
A Badger was the mascot, the colors orange and black.
Football was like religion. The town folk praised the team.
And if you were a player, you were held in high esteem.

A lot of things were happening at the Circus Drive In show
But they weren't on the big screen. They were happening
down below.
Down by the Pecos River or Old Maid Springs we'd park
So we could spend the evening and kiss there after dark.

There were historic places where one could take a hike,
Or travel ten miles out of town if you could ride a bike.
Castle Gap was halfway on the road to Crane
And there was Horsehead Crossing that watered wagon
trains.

Treasure hunters gather for a story that's oft retold
Of how a band of Indians stole Maximilian's gold.
And drove the laden wagons through the Crossing towards
the Gap,
Where they in turn were set upon by marauders in a trap.

When one is hunting arrowheads and looking at the ground
Occasionally there's a glitter of a Spanish coin that's found.
Dinosaurs left their muddy tracks near the road that's
headed west.
Where wildcatters find the oil and heavily invest.

Much closer and just east of town we have Humble Oil to
thank
For building oil storage that's a million barrel tank.
A concrete bowl for playground for a folly that went bad
When the concrete it expanded and drained all the oil it had.

At night we were surrounded by fires on King Mountain
That burned the sour gases. It was something you could
count on.
At times you'd smell the gases and thought that it was funny
To tell the one you're riding with "Well, dear, just smell the
money."

The only trees that grew there in the searing desert heat
Were really scraggly bushes that I learned were called
mesquite.
When I had just arrived there I saw something that amazes.
I watched from Badger stadium the rattlesnakey races.

My cousin, Joyce, would drive me if her father would allow
And ask me if I wanted a pink or purple cow.
At first I wasn't certain. What I expected was the worst.
But a cherry or a grape float would quench the summer
thirst

I remember Pansy, the local character
Who lived still in McCamey and all the kids feared her.
She had been a beauty, an athlete to admire
Who was a star attraction as she walked on the high wire.

I'll write another story about her circus act
And how she fell from up there and nearly broke her back.
Sometimes she'd pull her wagon as she walked about
Sometimes 'twas overflowing with the junk that she'd
checkout.

The girls were quite exciting from Joyce to Mary Lou,
Becky, Judy, Patsy, Donna, and LaDonna too.
Marilyn and May Carol, Mary, Billie Fay,
Beverly, Gayle, and Nancy I remember to this day.

Sharon, Paula, Barri, Barbara, and Bonnie Sue.
I stored them in my memory. What else was I to do?
My hometown was a garden of yellow Texas roses.
An oasis in the desert and fragrance for our noses.

You cannot put me on the spot to name my favorite.
There are still more I admired, Margaret, Trudy, and Jeanette.
I loved to watch the Badger Band with Majorettes so fine,
Especially when the times had changed and raised the skirt
hemline.

Sometimes when summer break would come and it would
start to swelter
I'd go across the alley and meet in a bomb shelter.
Sometimes I'd walk across the street and ten blocks to the
pool
To talk with bathing beauties and hoped that I was cool.

I loved the Baptist churches and going on retreats.
And I enjoyed the music of the band that played, Night
Beats.
I respected Sammy Long's advice and thought that he was
super
At keeping order and the law as our local Texas Trooper.

McCamey had an airport with service from El Paso.
Trans-Texas Airways used to stop, or so the old folks say so.
Runway 10 was the main one with forty one hundred feet.
Runway 28 one fourth of that, twelve fifty to where they
meet.

Some friends were going fishing and I clearly was invited.
My parents wouldn't let me go and I thought I was slighted.
I learned from them when they returned, but first I have to warn ya,
That they went fishing cross the border for strippers in Villa Acuna.

My mother taught the fourth grade, my dad cleaned the high school.
One thing that I remember, they preached the golden rule.
Though we weren't rich we had enough by common family measure.
The times I had, the things I did, are surely mine to treasure.

My memories of my hometown still echo in my mind
It was another era and everyone was kind.
A place where people spoke the truth and never told a lie.
I'm still a bloomin' Badger until the day I die.

MILLION BARREL OIL TANK

By Roy E. Peterson (April 4, 2012)

Two monumental errors were built from faulty plans
One next to McCamey and one at Monahans.
Two million barrel oil tanks were laid out in concrete,
But Shell forgot to calculate expansion and the heat.

The engineers had failed to check the underground substrata
They should have drilled to check the base and calculate the
data.
Underneath the heavy structure they would have limestone
found
That was not conducive to support the tanks on ground.

Shell had so much oil coming from their new found fields.
While every well they dug was shallow, they had
tremendous yields.
The mammoth oil reservoirs were built for surplus oil,
But in their haste to store it they forget to test the soil

Oil trucks hauled in tanks full of crude by day and night.
Until they could build a pipeline, they thought it was alright.
Shell built a wooden roof to cover all the oil inside,
But could fill them only part way up no matter how they
tried.

The concrete and the heavy oil crushed the limestone base
And then the trucks were used to load the oil back in their
space.
The leaks were from the bottom and from the sides as well
Two million barrel follies that had been built by Shell.

They had to stop production, and try to cut the yield
Until a pipeline could be built to Houston from the field.
There was no good solution to repair the damage done.
So now the empty oil tanks sit staring at the sun.

They look just like a stadium built 80 years ago,
And kids still like to party there and sometimes shoot their ammo.
Someday I'd like to buy it and with a little toil
I'd bring an oil rig in and drill for all that oil.

PART VIII

MY LOVE POEMS

Antique Valentine Photo

FINDING YOUR LOVE

By Roy E. Peterson (1962)

The night was dark, the rain came down
And then I heard the thunder.
They said I had been Suzy's clown.
She tore my heart asunder.

Your one true love is hard to find,
But she is worth the waiting.
Sometimes you almost lose your mind
Like you never did before.

Each one you love you want her to
Be your one and only.
But she walks out and makes you blue
Then you're so sad and lonely.

To find true love you look for her
You never cease your praying.
You'll find her at the rainbow's end,
Where the angels have been staying.

WISHING

By Roy E. Peterson (1962)

So sweet, so pretty, so sincere;
Growing more beautiful each passing year.
Each day adds blessings on you so young
Till someday you'll hear of your loveliness sung
By those who are seeking to hold your hand.
If you love them better, I'll understand.

CUP OF LOVE

By R. Eugene Peterson (1968)

At last you came from shrouded mist
That hid your beauty from my sight.
No more my strong imagination
Born of loneliness and night.

When red of autumn blazes glory
In crimson challenge to the cold,
Our love will burn like wine of vintage
In the cup of life we hold.

Again we'll drink of Life's clear fountain.
From golden chalice, drain love's wine.
We'll review remembered passion
And return to summertime.

To winter's blast fling taunts defiant
With autumn leaves be glorified.
Drink with me of Fates gold goblet.
Let our love be verified.

PRECIOUS PROMISES: NOW WE'RE ENGAGED

By Roy E. Peterson (January 2011)

Now we're engaged and the world must know
We're a couple in spirit wherever we go.
A circle of two when we put on the ring
We gave to each other our everything.

The past is behind us and future ahead
We dream of each other when we go to bed.
We're focused together on things we must do
To prepare for our wedding and starting anew.

Engagement has strengthened our love and our will.
Now we're united our dreams to fulfill.
No matter what else, we already are one
In vision, in planning, in doing, in fun.

To our friends we say thank you for just being there.
Old flames are extinguished. We no longer care.
Our marriage is coming our wedding will be
Our final binding for eternity.

LOVE IN THE AFTERGLOW

By Roy E. Peterson (March 2012)

As surely as the morning comes your future's looking bright,
But there will be those tougher times as surely comes the
night.
The strength of love is certain. It weighs the pros and cons.
A temple made of diamonds that's stronger than the bronze.

When two hearts are in unison they know that deep within
The fire of love is burning though patience's wearing thin.
They work it out together and add another layer
Of armor on their marriage, as they embrace in prayer.

The fragrance from their union is something to behold
Far sweeter than the orchids, or even of the rose.
A fountain everlasting that flows from God above
Will always keep it blooming, for they have planted love.

LIFE AND DEATH OF JEANNIE

By Roy E. Peterson November 11, 2012)

Who could foresee? Who could foretell
    My mournful tale I'll tell to thee
That inhabits my cortex and makes a hell
    Of my miserable life remaining to me.
My love's life expired on a warm summer night
    When an accident wounded her mortally.
    When I lost the touch of my fair JEANNIE.

On a grassy lawn by an ivied wall
    She thrilled to my hands wandering aimlessly
Beneath the sill of the darkened hall
    We explored each other incessantly
Until the warmth of the new daylight
    Revealed where we hid furtively;
    Exposed us arching fervently.

Summer vacation stole her away;
    She died in a car wreck unnaturally.
As always I called and was asked to pray
    By her parents crying portentously.
What happened I asked them both forthright?
    She lost her life sometime today.
    I sensed that Jeannie was not okay
    At exactly the minute she passed away.

Her auburn hair and her beautiful face
    Were lost to me that fateful day.
Her curvaceous body I always did trace
    Eroding in Death in whose throes she lay.
    Yet I saw her walk in the pale moonlight
    An hour or two after turning midnight.

The nights spent down on the grassy lawn
    Feed the images of my memory.
The time we spent before greeting the dawn
    Coming up on the periphery,
Endlessly soaring, taking flight.
    Night affects extra sensory
    Perceptions uncontrollably
    Leading to my insanity.

In my last will and testament
    I ask to be buried by my JEANNIE
In a sepulcher concrete encasement
    Residing together gravely
Basking in ghostly shadow light,
    Lying as one eternally;
    Sweet release infernally;
    Spirit infusing my JEANNIE.

PART IX

MY HUMOR

Charlie Chaplain Eating His Shoe
Classic Movie Photo

HOW TO HIT UPON A GIRL

By Roy E. Peterson (2006)

They told me "Hit upon a girl." I think I knocked her
senseless.
Should I have used a baseball bat to knock her through the
fences?
I thought I'd try a softer tact and make her ego swell.
But all I got was dirty looks and said she wasn't well.
I think the problem was the bat. I think that she was mad.
That I had hit her in the head with all the force I had.

LOVE MY SODA IN A BOTTLE

By Roy E. Peterson (2006)

I ain't drunk. I'm in love with my bottle.
I touch your lips and I'm goin' full throttle.
I caress your neck and hold your body,
While some of my friends are gettin' rowdy.

I drink of your courage. It sets me on fire.
I feel myself getting' higher and higher.
And when you're empty, it's really no bother.
I say soda jerk, just give me another.

SOUTHERN REBEL

By Roy E. Peterson (2006)

I'm a Southern Rebel. My head is on the level.
I eat grits and black-eyed peas.
My sled she runs on moonshine and flies across the ridgeline
Leavin' revenoors gasping in the trees.

I SHOT AN ARROW

(True Childhood Foibles)
By Roy E. Peterson (2006)

I shot an arrow in the air
It came to rest in mother's hair
She thought the Indians had gone wild,
But it was just her loving child.

I dropped the marbles in the soup.
I thought 'twas funny—ploop, ploop, ploop, ploop.
Down through the register from up on high
I'm glad I missed the pumpkin pie.

Roy Roger's stamp with brand of ink
I stamped the couch, what do you think.
When I got spanked I did admit,
I was the one who had done it.

I broke the wood collection plate
In half, before the service. It was great.
I pressed it back together and thought
It ought to hold, but I was wrong.

The usher passed the plate around,
And soon there was a thudding sound.
The usher had a funny smile,
While coins rolled all about the aisle.

Roger and I found the grape juice can.
We began to drink it like a man.
The juice that was poured for church communion
Brought us into laughing union.

We pretended we got drunk
And then we heard a heavy thunk.
Our mothers found us acting dumb
And hit upon us like a drum.

Riley and I got in my wagon
The old one with suspension draggin'.
The metal where the tongue had cut,
Was sharp in front and near my butt.

We went sailing anyway
Down past the fields of new mown hay.
Only halfway down the hill
The wagon stopped, we took a spill.

With me in front and Riley back
We both landed with a whack.
The metal ripped my pants in two,
I was unscathed, what should we do?

I put on my second pair
And down the hillside we did tear.
Again we made a sudden stop
And we went flying like a mop.

My second pair of jeans was split.
I feared my mother would have a fit.
She started laughing when she saw
That my rear end was getting raw.

Cousin Linda on her bike
Went flying past my little trike.
I lassoed her about the head
And when I pulled, thought she was dead.

Linda landed with a thud
Her fall was cushioned by farm lane mud.
She didn't know whether to laugh or cry,
As mother helped her to get dry.

Linda said she didn't know
That I had aim enough to throw
The little loop around her neck,
And now her bike, it was a wreck.

ODE TO TOILET PAPER

By Roy E. Peterson (February 1, 2012)

When I was young and needed to wipe,
A Sears catalog page I would swipe
Across my bottom, but I would need
Several pages to complete the deed.

At the age of 13 we moved to town
And catalog pages would not go down
The porcelain fixture in the little room,
So toilet paper became the norm.

Modern kids will not understand
My love for toilet paper in my hand.
They really can't appreciate
That toilet paper can feel so great.

Oh, toilet paper how I love thee!
I use one sheet when I have to pee.
I think of you as a soft tree bough.
What would I do without you now?

I take several sheets and fold in two
To clean up the other thing I do.
And if I happen to cut myself,
I reach for you upon the shelf.

I don't care if you're pink or blue.
Just plain white will surely do.
I want to thank you for being there.
You're something all my friends can share.

DON'T YOU THINK IT IS A CRIME WHEN A POEM DOESN'T RHYME

By Roy E. Peterson (October 9, 2012)

Don't you think it is a crime when a poem doesn't rhyme?
Like a discordant chime ringing three-quarter time?
I condemn the poet who has nary a clue
How to rhyme with me or you. What are we supposed to do?
Poets should aspire to more. Lack of effort I abhor.
So to poets I implore, give me something to adore.

Don't you think it is a waste when an artist has no taste?
Modern art should be erased. It already looks defaced.
I decry the works of all paintings hanging on a wall
Like those painted by Warhol who my senses appall.
Artists should be made to paint something beautiful and quaint.
So to artists here's my plaint, give me something more than paint.

Don't you think there's something wrong, when they call a rap a song?
Where's my hook and where's my gong? There's no way it can belong.
How I hate the rapper rapping with his mouth flap, flap, flapping,
Volume on the speaker ramping to the max the sound is amping.
Music needs a melody, or it is a felony.
So musicians here's my plea, trash the rap insulting me.

FRACTURED BIRTHDAY GREETINGS

By Roy E. Peterson (June 24, 2012)

Money's tight and times are hard,
So I'm sending you this card.

I'm sending you this birthday wish,
At your age you forgot about it.

For all the candles on your cake,
You needn't an oven for it to bake.

The lavender that grows in France
Won't smell as good as your birthday pants.

Another birthday, how can it be
That you don't even remember me?

So many candles, so little cake.
A bigger one I'll have to make.

As your best friend who is tried and true,
I'm telling that time's running out on you.

'Tis better to realize you're over the hill,
Than be buried beside your favorite still.

It matters not the twists of fate,
But can you sneak inside the Pearly Gate.

May birthday wishes flow like wine.
Just don't try to get drunk this time.

WHEN ALL ELSE FAILS

By Roy E. Peterson (May 20, 2012)

When all else fails, pull the plug
Or maybe sweep it under the rug.
Maybe a coat of paint will work
Or maybe sell it to some jerk.

When all else fails, admit she's right
Saves some time; avoids a fight.
One can simply tell the boss.
Good idea to cover loss.

When all else fails, the Gremlins did it.
Blame someone else, another dimwit.
Maybe Marie or the dunce you call Teddy.
In any case have a good excuse ready.

When all else fails, change the pro rata.
Manipulate well the statistical data.
Maybe it just wasn't meant to be
Like asking your dog to live in a tree.

HOW I GOT DIVORCED

By Roy E. Peterson (October 2012)

My wife got dressed up for a party and asked for my
opinion
I said,
"If we are going to a fight, you've made the right decision."
I bled.

While eating ice cream my wife said, "I hope I won't get fat."
Guess what!
"Too late," I said and ducked as it hit the window with a
splat!
I'm a nut.

While putting makeup on my wife remarked, "I needed
this."
I heard.
When I agreed, I should have known her aim just couldn't
miss.
Awkward!

My Army Colonel made us officers put condoms in our kit.
The story's true.
To handout to enlisted free. She threw a tantrum fit.
I was black and blue.

While on a business trip someone took my picture with a
hottie.
What luck!
They gave it to my wife; she thought that I was being
naughty.
I got stuck.

I learned a lot in thirty years of marriage to my wife.
Of course.
It could have been much worse though. I could have lost my
life,
But divorce.

YOU WARPED ME

By Roy E. Peterson (August 5, 2012)

You warped me for life, you warped me real good.
I should have stayed out of your neighborhood.
You were so hot, I thought you were cool.
You bent over backwards, I broke every rule.

How could I know I'd be putty in your hand?
I was just clueless and did not understand
That you were magic and put on a hex.
Now I am warped and my nickname is Flex.

Don't get me wrong I am satisfied
You never pretended and you never lied.
I just didn't know what you'd do to me.
The things I would do. The things I would see.

The only drug was your sweet perfume
That assaulted my senses with you in the room.
No alcohol, but I'm intoxicated
By thinking of you and the ways we related.

You warped my senses with your imagery.
Who would have thought of such deviltry?
My thoughts are vivid, my mind is racy.
I'm looking forward to real intimacy.

FACEBOOK FOLLIES

By Roy E. Peterson (July 30, 2012)

My finger gets too numb to "like" every post that's there.
What has been seen can't be "unseen"." What is done is done.
I unfriended half my friends and no one seemed to care.
If I can write a smarter quote, then I think I've won.

Friend's pictures may be older than you think they really are.
Some friends agree with what you wrote, some cannot comprehend.
Friends of friends that you don't know may judge you from afar.
People you don't know can read what you did not intend.

If a friend you think you know skips a month or two,
Don't give up and don't panic, they still may be alive.
Be careful what you write or post about the things you do.
Remember what you say or do exists in someone's archive.

A "friend" may be a figment of the imagination.
Some cannot be understood. For others you've a feel.
Typo's get mistaken for an abbreviation.
A friend may be illusory, but a relative is real.

A Social Network's fine I guess for Generation Y.
A newsfeed filled by photos, sometimes there's good advice;
Instant gratification and candy for the eye.
Salacious gossip rampant sharing, such a fun device.

What more could all the denizens wish happily each day
Than be connected to their sphere of faithful worshipers?
Where else can one make contact with friends that want to play?
A group of masqueraders and authors without borders.

KING DAVID

By Roy E. Peterson (June 22, 2012)

My cousin, Dr/Rev Roy Backus asked on his weekly "Got 60 Seconds" message, "What is the primary positive attribute of King David?" I wrote:

> Young David was a good rock hound
> He chose superb ones hard and round.
> His aim was straight with his sling shot.
> Killed Goliath on the spot.
>
> As a shepherd kept his sheep
> Safe from harm. Sang them to sleep.
> Picked to be a future king.
> Rock star musician when he'd sing.
>
> Was a poet. Good harpist.
> Was King Saul's own therapist.
> Soothed King Saul as he did ask.
> That was not an easy task.
>
> Played games with the King's own son.
> Hide and seek with Jonathan.
> Dodged a javelin from King Saul
> Thrown at him near palace wall.
>
> Must have been an architect.
> House of David did erect.
> An attribute for his selection
> Was comely face and good reflection.
>
> Good at asking God's forgiveness
> After all he had experience
> But the thing that stood apart,
> He was "a man after God's own heart."

FILL MY FACEBOOK

By Roy E. Peterson (December 4, 2012)

Fill my Facebook newsfeed daily,
Falalalalalalalala.
Tis the season to go crazy,
Falalalalalalalala.
Don we now our Christmas sweater,
Falala, Falala, lalala.
Shop the mall in any weather,
Falalalalalalalala.

See the blazing car behind us,
Falalalalalalalala.
Struck the hydrant join the chorus,
Falalalalalalalala.
One less shopper for that treasure
Falalalalalalalala
Give's me that much greater pleasure
Falalalalalalalala.

Sing the songs all hale and hearty,
Falalalalalalalala
Kiss the girls at Christmas Party.
Falalalalalalalala.
After Christmas comes the New Year,
Falalalalalalalala.
Stick it in your blooming ear,
Falalalalalalalala.

PUBLICUS

By Roy E. Peterson (December 3, 2012)

A peaceful day! Do not disturb!
No promises! Do not perturb!
No messages! No telephone!
At last I think I am alone.

I'll take a name, a nom de plume
A clever one I will assume.
Guess what I wrote upon the page?
The Writer of the Purple Sage.

But Publicus is better yet
For all the people I have met.
A few I love. A few I hate.
But most of them are really great.

The word means public actuary.
I read it in the dictionary.
A clever name for Everyman
A new career I thus began.

I like to have a cover name
No one can find who they should blame.
So Publicus will be just fine
A name that's candid, yet benign.

DISAPPEARING INK

By Roy E. Peterson (December 3, 2012)

I just bought a book on invisibility
A thing that's difficult in today's society.
I laid it on the counter to read it later on,
But when I went to look for it
I thought that it was gone.

I felt around and found it and just like holding air
My hands were spread apart, but it looked like nothing there.
I went to read the words and then what do you think?
The book must have been written
In disappearing ink.

I wish upon some people invisibility.
Who're lacking in their manners with no civility.
Especially the tattooed ones and those who like to drink.
I'd love to give a bottle of
Some disappearing ink.

PART X

MY HOLIDAYS

A Song for the Seasons Painting
by Jane Scott Wooster

A FURTIVE VALENTINE

By Roy E. Peterson (February 14, 2012)

I would have sent you roses.
I would have sent a card.
But how would you explain them?
I think it would be hard.

My message is what matters.
A Valentine's Day thought.
A secret kept between us.
More than I could have bought.

Furtive hugs and kisses
Have passed throughout the year
In messages like this one
And words that I revere.

Though miles are far between us
And years have passed away,
Another hug I send you.
On this red roses day.

IMPISH IRISH AND ST PATRICK'S DAY

By Roy E. Peterson (March 17, 2012)

From Donegal to old Killarney
Irish have the gift of Blarney.
Whether angel, whether rogue
I love to hear them speak their brogue.

I'd love to have a leprechaun
With pot o' gold stored on my lawn.
Rainbows always ending there.
For luck o' the Irish the gold he'd share

I wish my dog were an Irish Rover
And shamrocks grew like four leaf clover.
A Celtic lass with her red tresses
Flowing softly o'er her dresses.

I'd love to see the Emerald Isle
And Celtic women that beguile.
Then I'd like to eat and ravage
A dinner of corned beef and cabbage.

I'd like to learn what drove Oscar Wilde.
Was it the authors he profiled?
A well known author in his day
He wrote "The Picture of Dorian Gray."

Why did Bram Stoker write "Dracula"?
The police in Ireland carry a shillelagh?
Perhaps one evening down at the pub
I'd sing "Danny Boy" without a flub.

MEMORIAL DAY 1955

By Roy E. Peterson (April 6, 2012)

I recall Memorial Day in nineteen fifty five.
The little auditorium was filled with those alive
Who soldiered through a World War and then Korea, too.
Who loved their native country and flag, red, white, and blue.

I lived in the Dakotas in a town called Bonesteel.
Just before the program I heard the church bells peal.
The high school band was the parade there wasn't any more.
When they marched in to City Hall, the veterans closed the door.

A poppy cost a penny, a crimson paper flower
That wrapped around my button like everybody wore.
Mother sang the anthem and when the taps were played
My dad led all the veterans in a salute and prayed.

A roll call of the veterans, those who served and died,
Was read by an old Chaplain as family members cried.
Four coffins represented the different wars we fought.
The Civil and the World Wars, and Korea as they ought.

Then families got in their cars and went to visit graves
Adorned with cross and flowers and flags that blew in waves.
The veterans fired their rifles as the casings fell in grass.
Then kids like me got busy and picked up all the brass.

A glorious time to be a boy to watch the grand procession.
A happy time without a war and over the depression.
A time when patriots hearts still beat and passed it on to me.
Duty, honor, country. Liberty's not free.

Then we got together and met at grandpa's place.
Riley, Nola, Linda, and Karen and I said grace.
We had been playing hide and seek and had to wash our hands
In one of those old basins on one of those old stands.

While Uncles Ray and Dale with Dad and Grandpa hit
The croquet ball through wicker hoops with colored wooden mallet,
Aunts Cecil and Luella with Mom and Grandma too
Would fill the table full of food just like they used to do.

I wonder if in those small towns in places like Dakota,
Nebraska, Kansas, Iowa, and those in Minnesota,
Still honor vets who sacrificed their very life for all
The rest of us now living as their memories we recall.

FALL FANTASY

By Roy E. Peterson (October 7, 2012)

Come the dread night shadows creeping, filtering curtains barely keeping
Misty moonlight beams from seeping through the room and to the hall.
Ghostly demons float unending, messages to me are sending
Echoes from the past resounding, bouncing off my wall.
Bouncing, sounding, mind confounding are resounding
Hardly heard, and that is all.

Wide awake within an instant, though the echoes sounded distant
Still it seemed that they were rampant like a demonic call.
Wondered what they were intending, could it be that they were wending
Their way home along my wall, coming from a Monster Ball?
Worried next what might be pending, maybe my downfall
Darkness then with no recall.

Dare I draw the purple curtain, hesitant and still uncertain,
Fearful finding fetid villain perched upon my stony wall
That encloses my estate. Maybe swinging on my gate.
Maybe drinking at my fountain. Hugging gloom amidst the pall.
Changing shapes and standing tall, shadow cross my country sprawl
Laughing hard, the ghouls enthrall.

As I peered out on Halloween, playful demons in muted scene,
Flitted round the neighbor's green dancing at a ghoulish ball.
Visions of the past were flashing as the goblin hordes were dancing.

Dancing, prancing, quite entrancing playful in a light snowfall.
Echoes of a distant call, bonfire burned in my eyeball.
Swirling leaves from oak trees fall.

HALLOWEEN TRICK

By Roy E. Peterson (November 1, 2012)

Gave out no candy this Halloween;
No buttercup and no jelly bean.
Locked up my door and latched up my screen.
Neighborhood kids think that I am mean.

Hung out a sign upon my tree—
Bet that you can't toilet paper me!
Sat in the dark and laughingly
Figured the best things in life are free.

Checked in the morning what do you guess?
Out on my lawn was quite a mess;
My sign had been a complete success.
A hundred rolls or more, not less.

No angry words and I showed no fear.
Toilet paper up there and here.
Thought to myself it does appear
Enough toilet paper to last me a year.

HALLOWEEN 2012

By Roy E. Peterson (October 31, 2012)

Got dressed up for Halloween
Scariest costume kids had seen.
If you ask, what could it be?
My answer is I dressed as me.

If my friends think I am scary,
It's the moon that made me hairy.
Had to hide upon the roof.
People searched for the werewolf.

Neighbors searching far and wide;
Want to tan a werewolf's hide.
They'll never track me to my den.
When sun comes up I'm me again.

THANKSGIVING 2012

By Roy E. Peterson (November 22, 2012)

Thanksgiving comes but once a year
Soon I'll stuff the turkey's rear.
Cook till it is golden browned.
My giblet gravy is renowned.

Mashed potatoes, candy yams,
Chestnut stuffing made with clams,
French's® green bean casserole,
And butter for my dinner roll.

I'll give a sparkling cider toast
To the one's that I love most.
A good Thanksgiving it would seem
With pumpkin pie and whipping cream.

Before I eat I'll say a prayer
For everyone for whom I care.
Listen to a football game
And later I will eat the same.

After I have cooked the best,
Thanksgiving is my day of rest.
When the evening shadows creep,
Tryptophan will help me sleep.

FIRST OF DECEMBER

By Roy E. Peterson (December 1, 2012)

First of December—see you soon Santa.
Perhaps we could share a drink of Mylanta.
The corn's in the corncrib
The hay's in the mow.
What kind of year did you have anyhow?

First of December—I hope it was good.
The criminal boss is still running our hood.
He got reelected.
Can you believe that?
I'm looking all over cause I smell a rat.

First of December—I went to the store.
I stood in the line, but was stuck at the door.
Who are these people
And why are they here?
I guess welfare checks are much better this year.

CHRISTMAS LETTER 2009

By Roy E. Peterson (December 1, 2009)

Merry Christmas 2009 to all!
May you recover from the shopping mall.
Looked at the Internet, shopped real hard,
But they would not accept my credit card.

I'm not dreaming of a white Christmas.
Think of the snow. Think of the fuss.
Here in California it would just be nice
To have a green Christmas without any ice.

Mom is 94 now and does not know
Whether there's wind out, or rain, or snow.
I call every week, but she plays a game
That she does not even remember my name.

Kids are grown now and far away.
What shall I do this Christmas day?
Drink non-alcoholic eggnog and watch TV
Maybe watch football, I'll have to see.

What did I do this year you say?
Worked real hard without any pay.
Still plan to make it big out here.
I hope to succeed this coming year.

IF THERE WERE NO CHRISTMAS

By Roy E. Peterson (December 2010)

If there were no Christmas, where would we be?
No tinsel, no light strings, no evergreen tree.
No one to show us the way we should go
With mercy for travelers who drive through the snow.

If there were no Christmas, when would we give gifts?
Who'd brave the blizzards? Who'd cut through the drifts?
Where'd be the carolers singing their songs
Of peace and goodwill and forgiveness for wrongs?

If there were no Christmas, then just tell me this—
Who'd hang the mistletoe, who'd give me a kiss?
Who'd play at Santa and deliver the toys
To good little girls and good little boys?

If there were no Christmas and Christ was not born,
We'd be little lost sheep all alone and forlorn.
We'd have no more model of humility
By one who was born so he'd die on a tree.

So keep Christ in Christmas, the least we can do
And keep giving presents for me and for you.
In memory of Christ the child who was brave
And came down to earth our souls to save.

I'LL NEVER FORGET THE CHRISTMAS

By Roy E. Peterson (December 2010)

I'll never forget the Christmas we still talk about,
When stockings caught fire and made children shout.
When father climbed upon the roof to hang lights on the
eaves
And fell off of the ladder in a pile of leaves.

I'll never forget the Christmas the needles got dry
They fell off the Christmas tree and made mother sigh.
Who spiked the punch and got everyone drunk
And crashed on the table, now who'd ever thunk.

I never saw such kissing beneath the mistletoe.
I never heard such smooching as we watched the show.
While aunts and uncles thought they were Santa Claus
We kids had all decided, to save our kitty, Paws.

I'll never forget the Christmas that set off a roar
When mom dropped the turkey and stuffing on the floor.
The cat was very happy to lick up all the grease
And then my aunt came crying as she burned up all the
peas.

I'll never forget the Christmas the fireworks were stored
Behind the tree for New Years. 'Twas quite a hoard.
And as it neared evening, Dad plugged the socket in.
At first came a sizzle, and then a big din.

It must have been wire the cat chewed we learned
That started first sparking, then needles got burned.
Which set the box of fireworks ablaze in all their glory
I laugh when I relate this and tell you the story.

We quickly ducked for cover as a rocket hit the wall
The next struck the ceiling and plaster to fall.
Then to our amazement the Roman candles lit.
We crawled into the parlor, so we would not get hit.

I'll ne'er forget that Christmas as relatives went home.
They couldn't us leave fast enough and soon we were alone.
My parents started laughing what else could they do.
What a memorable Christmas! I began laughing too.

CHRISTMAS LETTER 2012

By Roy E. Peterson (November 30, 2012)

Every year I feel the need to write a Christmas letter.
Some friends think I'm getting worse. While others think I'm better.
Some cousins think I lost it all. Some cousins think I'm rich.
I'm really somewhere in between the roadway and the ditch.

What have you done this year is the question you all ask?
Did your life have meaning? Did you fulfill your task?
Did you get some presents? Or give a bunch away?
What will you be doing on this snowy Christmas Day?

I wrote a lot of poetry and read a book or two.
I authored one book of my own before I caught the flu.
I moved back home to Tucson and settled down again.
I went back to California a wedding to attend.

My son came twice to visit. He brought his lovely bride.
The first time to the hospital, because I almost died.
The second time was wonderful, since here I am an expert
We visited Mt Lemmon and the museum of the desert.

My mother in West Texas is ninety-seven now.
I call her every Sunday and try to talk somehow.
She can't remember very much. The nurse I keep addressing.
I traveled there to see her. That was my yearly blessing.

My Christmas will be silent. No jingle bells or mouse.
Alone I'll eat my dinner for now I have no spouse.
No presents left by Santa. No tap of tiny hoof.
No reindeer are expected dancing on my roof.

My children have all married with families of their own.
Perhaps someone will call me upon the telephone.
Grandkids will be happy with money that I send.
I know it isn't very much; it's all that I can spend.

NEW YEARS EVE

By Roy E. Peterson (December 31, 2012)

Soon the past year ledger closes.
Challenges the New Year poses.
Prickly thorns or fragrant roses?
Ready for what life proposes.

Made a list of resolutions.
Some of them are just illusions.
Others may be just delusions
Taken from my own confusions.

Every year I make a checklist.
Approach each year an optimist.
I'm sure some things will still persist,
But hope bad habits I'll resist.

Looking through my photo albums
Till the midnight hour welcomes
With joyful shouts upon my eardrums
Everyone with their own customs.

Fireworks outside my window
Set the midnight sky aglow.
Sit alone and watch the show.
Had no need for mistletoe.

Another day another year.
Have to make another prayer
That the loved ones I hold so dear
Are free from want and free from fear.

PART XI

MY MYSTICAL MOMENTS

Untitled

I BELIEVE IN ANGELS

By Roy E. Peterson (February 7, 2012)

I believe in Angels. In fact I've known a few.
I dedicate my words to them for everything they do.
I know I kept them busy just looking after me.
How many Angels do you ask? I think its
twenty-three.

I AM YOUR GUARDIAN ANGEL

By Roy E. Peterson (January 2011)

I am your Guardian Angel now in everything you do.
I'll give you strength to carry on. I'm never far from you.
Just say a little prayer at work, or place that you may be.
Then I'll destroy the evil ones and make the demons flee.

I am your Guardian Angel sent down to help you cope
With those who want to bring you down and take away your
      hope.
Yes, I am on a mission here to keep you safe from harms
And save you for the one you love who waits with open
      arms.

I know you've felt my presence as I touched your inner soul.
The times when danger lingered near and I have kept you
      whole.
"Oh, Thank you Guardian Angel," was all the praise I need,
To touch me while I'm watching, and keep you safe indeed.

I am your Guardian Angel. I know you've felt my hand.
If there is danger lurking near, I call an angel band
To put their wings around you and keep you safe and warm.
I am a mighty warrior who can miracles perform.

Now please just pray to Jesus and He will talk to God.
He'll send a bolt of lightning and use his mighty rod.
The demons cannot hurt you or work when he is mad.
He'll use His heavenly powers to cast away the bad.

I came here to protect you. I am God's messenger.
I whisper softly to you, but I'm an avenger
To fight the hosts of Satan's hell, bent on deviltry
And cut the bonds of evil to set God's people free.

COUNTER INVICTUS?

By R. Eugene Peterson (1962)

Out of the light that guides me
Down glorious pathways of gold
I thank the God I know to be
For my unconquerable soul.

Love is the anchor of circumstance.
I shall not wince, or furl my brow.
Under the rule that men call chance
I've found the secret of happiness now.

Beyond this sorrow filled veil of tears
Someday we'll move toward lengthening shade.
Regardless the specter of the years
He'll find us loving and unafraid.

I have no fear how narrow the gate,
For marked upon eternity's scroll
Are these few words revealing our fate,
"Two hearts stand here—they make a soul."

THOUGH WORLDS MAY DIE AND SILENT BE

By Roy E. Peterson (Unknown date)

Till rolling seas cease heaving high;
The starry nights stop passing by;
The universe is wrapped in flame;
And there is no one left to blame;
Until then? You're my loved one.

Till sun no longer makes a day;
And earth will never get a ray;
The quiet coldness of the earth;
Bespeaks a lonely universe;
Until then? I'm still not done.

Though worlds may die and silent be
We still have an eternity
To be together on and on.
The words like death and dying gone.
Until then? Our love has just begun.

SOMEONE WHO WASN'T THERE

By Roy E. Peterson (March 8, 2012)

My publisher told me face to face
Find somewhere with lots of space.
Concentrate, pick up the pace.
Somewhere hidden as your base.

The agent in the plunging blouse
Said to me, "I've just the house!"
Belonged to someone name of Kraus
Who left it when he lost his spouse.

"It's fully furnished, as you request
The owner only bought the best.
You'll be a very welcome guest
And get some quiet, get some rest."

I surveyed the mansion that very day
Wrote out the check so I could pay.
My description if I had to say,
"An Impressionist painting by Monet."

The mansion sat in velvet hills
With gardens framed by daffodils.
I rented it and paid the bills,
But not for finding silly thrills.

The agent said, "I hope you'll find
This home will give you peace of mind."
"Please don't think I am unkind,
I did not come here to unwind."

"I'm an author. I need to write
Sometimes by day, sometimes at night."
The agent smiled and said, "All right.
I hope the ghosts don't give you fright!"

I watched her as she walked away;
Her derriere full throttle sway.
Images in my mind a play
I waved and said, "I thank you, Kay"

The mansion came with cook and maid
Some nights they left, some nights they stayed.
The elder cook looked half sautéed.
The comely maid her breasts displayed.

One night the cook and maid were gone.
I had to stifle back a yawn
I heard the rain through curtains drawn
But then the lightning hit the lawn.

While I was sipping pekoe tea
The thunder almost deafened me.
I think the lightning hit a tree.
I jerked the curtains back to see

Cleft in two the giant elm
Half pointed to another realm.
The senses seemed to overwhelm.
Unbridled captain at the helm.

As I peered on, the slithering rain
Beat upon my window pane.
An image mirrored to my brain
Perhaps I'm going quite insane.

As lightning once again hit ground,
Immediately I turned around.
'Tis hard to write down what a found.
An apparition without sound.

I saw someone who wasn't there.
A silhouette upon a chair.
A maiden with a vacant stare.
I didn't speak. I didn't dare.

A flash of lightning from the storm
The ectoplasm had a form.
The shape I saw did not conform
To anything that was the norm.

The maiden sat there in the nude.
I think she was in pensive mood.
You may think I am being crude,
But beauty cannot be called lewd.

She rubbed her hand between her thigh
And then she turned and caught my eye.
First with a shudder, then a sigh
She turned her face up to the sky.

Then with another thunder clap
I heard a crackle, then a snap
While wispy clouds of mist enwrap
My mind as if I'm in a trap.

Although I like to write romance,
I dared not take another glance.
I didn't want to take the chance
Of falling in another trance.

As for the telling, I'll defer.
Of this postponement I am sure.
Someday I'll tell my publisher
About the night I spent with her.

POE WOULD APPROVE

By Roy E. Peterson (March 9, 2012)

Poe's nightmares inhabiteth the senses
In the past and present tenses.
Sepulchers of death in stone engraven
Crested by the maddening "Raven".

Shadows upon darkness and mystery
Chased with intriguing poetry.
Indulge me as I reminisce
And take you close to the abyss.

First with "Premature Burial" we may start
And follow with "The Tell Tale Heart."
Next the "The Fall of the House of Usher,"
Followed by the "Purloined Letter."

"The Mask of the Red Death" strikes a chord
Then read "The Murders in the Rue Morgue.
"The Pit and the Pendulum" and "The Black Cat"
"A Descent into the Maelstrom" and things like that.

"The Gold-Bug," "The Imp of the Perverse,"
"The Cask of Amontillado," it's getting worse.
"The Oval Portrait" hanging there
Should give everyone a scare.

"Eldorado" and Annabel Lee"
"The Bells" and The City in the Sea."
"The Raven" and the lost "Lenore"
Will never be heard from anymore.

IN THE DARK OF THE NIGHT

By Roy Peterson (June 2011)

In the dark of the night when the moon's out of sight
The phantoms are free to approach even me.
They are probably right to stay out of the light
And not let me see they have hostility.

Ghosts prey on the brain. They're seeking to drain
My good energy like the sap from a tree.
It is really inane that they're acting insane.
Whether he or a she, it's encompassing me.

I must concentrate, when the time's getting late
And avoid their advances when they're casting trances.
Inspiration is great, but I refuse to relate
To their play that entrances and their silly romances.

I can't let them see, they are getting to me.
I keep my own vow to not raise my eyebrow.
It's a quarter to three, and they must let me be.
The ghosts anyhow must be leaving by now.

MY SOUL TO TAKE

By Roy E. Peterson (April 4, 2012)

A mind more powerful than mine compels me to write
Between sundown and sunup till dawn's early light.
I am driven by a force or forces that penetrate my cranium
From my cerebral cortex flows prose from the "subterraneum."

My semiconscious state contributes to the somnambulistic
Incantations reverberating inwardly as though they're heuristic
Guiding, instructing, demanding. I cannot stem the tide.
Am I a prisoner, or am I the warden? Where can I hide?

Both must exist in the same superstructure. If I could name
The muse that invades my soul that I'm seeking to tame
And who opens the channels of thought, I would tell you.
Perhaps a spirit vector morphing which I have to subdue.

I channel perceptions, clouded instructions of an ethereal being
Unambiguous, yet indecipherable images that I am seeing
Floating in and out of my reality, or unreality, as the case may be
A fascinating paragon of the past and future that both haunt me.

A mind numbing psychic phenomena just happened to me.
With channels of thought open and receptors operating free.
I felt an acute preternatural sense an email message was amiss.
Titled, "60 Seconds with God." Subtext, "Let's see if Satan can stop this."

Besides the text and subtext, the thought to check my email
Was simultaneous almost with the transmission detail.
This was not the first time I experienced a transcendental
Whisper or image from that source and I'm being factual.

It was the first time she forwarded a message to me this way.
There wasn't anything I could send back to her or say.
The incongruity with the darker muse shattered my tranquility
And left my mind to wander and perambulate mentally.

The Yin, the Yang; the Good, the Bad; the white, the black
Now I had two clearly defined opposites that I had to track.
It was like a dash of cold water in which my conscious state
Like an antenna acquired signals, which I sometimes relate.

PHANTOM GIRL IN MY DREAMS

By Roy E. Peterson (March 2011)

I saw her again in my dreams last night as clear as I'm writing
this now.
The girl in my dream I know is right, but I really don't know
how
To tell you the way she makes me feel, or where she could
ever be.
I only can tell you I know she's real and that she was meant
for me.

I have some clues that are in my mind and have to write them
down.
I'm praying some day that I will find her in that Southern
town.
She's not the model I had for her in my waking conscious
state.
The vision was strong and not a blur, but my time is getting
late.

I can start with the way she wore her hair: shoulder length
and straight.
Her skin translucent while sitting there. This is so hard to
relate.
Her slender face framed by perfumed hair cascading from her
head.
I really must try to get this right as I get up from my bed.

The love of my life has a modest laugh, not loud as some may
be.
A quiet laugh, like a photograph as if sharing a secret with
me.
She wore a white sweater I think was plain and had on tight
blue jeans.
The smile of a lifetime drove me insane as if in a movie
scene.

We physically hugged and then we knew what we had missed
so long.
Something inside that instantly grew and that we felt so
strong.
We were both divorced with children grown. I told her I had
four.
But all were gone now, none were home of that I'm very
sure.

I kissed her on her lovely lips the taste much sweeter than
wine.
Images like movie clips kept flipping through my mind.
I don't recall we even spoke, but a powerful love was there.
I felt the love when I awoke while playing with her hair.

Will she return again to me to tease me in a dream?
Or will she be reality, or in a movie scene?
Where will I find my phantom lady? The one I know is mine.
The one who's wearing denim and sweater cut so fine.

WHAT SWEET MADNESS

By Roy E. Peterson (March 2011)

What sweet madness overpowers my senses?
What great gladness from phantom caresses?
What joy and happiness my mind confesses?
You are the enchantress with magical essences.

When did I know that my heart was aglow?
When did it show that I wanted you so?
When did hello chisel on my tableau?
I felt the snow melt and lava to flow.

Where have you been? You're a perfect ten?
From whence come thou then? From the forest or glen?
Where yet again can I find your love den?
You're my perfect woman, and that's an amen.

Was it your perfume when you came in the room?
Was it your typhoon that sealed my doom?
Was it your dark plume of smoke in the gloom?
May I kiss your lips bloom ere I go to my tomb.

How did it transpire that I felt this hot fire?
How did I perspire as the flames leaped higher?
How did you inspire this intense desire?
You are the purveyor and I am the buyer.

Who shaped your hair on your face so fair?
Who can compare with such beauty so rare?
Who is aware of the things that you share?
You're my love affair, though its solitaire.

You're my Aphrodite in a diaphanous nighty.
You're my Venus brightly that burns so rightly.
You're my muse so mighty with body that's tightly.
Come to me nightly and make me feel lightly.

Did she come from the sea? Did she come just for me?
Is she my destiny for an eternity?
I am bound happily. I will never be free.
Through my madness I see, this was just meant to be.

Why do I dream? Are things just what they seem?
In the pale moonbeam there is so much steam?
Why does it gleam like a molten stream?
I want to scream from this ecstasy supreme.

THERE IS A SECRET GARDEN

By Roy E. Peterson (February 14, 2012)

There is a secret garden within my heart and soul
Where I have planted roses for all the love's I know.
The fragrance of my garden, when memory takes a stroll,
Pervades my inner senses, while visiting each row.

The yellow rose for Texas, the red ones for Virginia,
Entrancing blooming beauties await my admiration.
The white ones South Dakota, the pink for California.
A garden filled with roses all share my adulation.

If I could be a hummingbird, I'd flit among them all.
I'd sip their nectar carefully while hovering in space.
Then like a happy gardener I'd sit upon the wall
And drink in all the beauty as I surveyed the place.

My roses are preserved there. They never droop or fade.
Their perky petalled faces expecting my sweet kiss.
Whether in the sunlight, or whether in the shade,
My secret garden's beautiful, a scene of perfect bliss.

HEAVENLY BODY

By Roy E. Peterson (March, 2011)

My muse is quite entrancing, one of the heavenly beauties.
I thank the Lord while standing, or at night upon my knees.
One of the nine sweet sisters born of Zeus and Mnemosyne
The brightest star in heaven and she was made for me.

Is it Clio the Muse of history? It depends upon my writing.
Or perhaps it's the fair Calliope, protector of heroic sightings.
I know sometimes it's Erato, the muse of love's poetry.
Their inspiration opens the mind and purges my memory.

My mind is incessantly active. I never have drawn a blank.
Apparently my three main muses are drawn to my memory
bank.
I have never seen their faces, but sensed their powerful
charm
As one would affect what's written, while another guided
my arm.

GHOSTS OF OLD MHS

By Roy E. Peterson (November 15, 2012)

If you go real late at night
Looking for a ghostly fright,
To the halls of our old school
You will make the goblins drool.

If you go to our reunion
You may get your own contusion
Running from the sights you see.
Maybe you should let them be.

Who would want to haunt the hall
Where Ms. Baskett yelled, "You all
Get into my room right now,
But I may spank you anyhow!"

Mr. Miller won't be there
Sitting in his easy chair.
Many teachers left that place,
Who would not want to show their face.

I wonder who you think you'll see
Making out with ghostly me
Down the hall by my old locker.
You could be in for quite a shocker.

If a ghost goes limping by,
Promise me you will not cry.
After all the drinks you had,
Maybe it will be my dad.

PART XII

MY MEMORIES

Oak Alley Plantation Painting by Gene Ritchhart

I AM THE KEEPER OF MEMORIES

By Roy E. Peterson (February 11, 2012)

I am the Keeper of Memories in a scrapbook in my mind,
The senses there are quickened with snapshots I can find
Detailing in a second everyone I knew.
While flashing through the pages, I always think of you.

A rose within my garden can never smell as sweet
As memories I garnered and stored within my "Keep".
You are forever present and but a thought away.
I wish that I could tell you my memories some day.

The time will come I'm certain when memories left are few
Within the vaulted ceilings the etchings fade from view.
The time has come to write them so memories pass along
To all the ones who matter to make the paintings strong.

Out there beyond the sunset, when my days are done,
I still will keep your memory somewhere beyond the sun.
You may feel my presence in the breeze or by the trees
And then you may remember, I'm the Keeper of Memories.

IF I COULD GO BACK IN TIME

By Roy E. Peterson (September 16, 2011)

If I could go back in time again,
I wonder at things that might have been.
If I could exchange right now for then,
My world would change as I imagine.

I realize today just why and how
My life would be richer and fuller now.
And if the Lord would please allow,
A different lover, a stronger vow.

If I could go back to the fork in the road,
I would have carried a lighter load.
I would have been strong, I would have been bold.
But who then could say, who could have foretold?

I have been blessed. My life has been good.
I did all the things I thought I should.
But looking back where once I stood,
It could have been better, I know it could.

I'M YESTERDAYS FOOL

Song by Roy E. Peterson (February 7, 2012)

Chorus

I'm yesterday's fool for losing you.
It's all over now, I'll make it somehow
But what can I do.
I loved only you. And now we're through.
You did me wrong and now you're gone.

Verse 1

When I was in love sometime long ago
You were with me where ever I would go.
And I was sure our love would endure.
Our love was real for I could feel you in my soul.

Verse 2

What happened to us? What could it be
That caused us to set each other free?
And yet I have found that I was bound
I could not conceal the way that I feel for eternity.

Verse 3

My life filled with power, with riches, with things,
With golden pins, and jewels, and rings.
The things that I thought I never forgot.
It should have been you. I hadn't a clue what you would do.

A BIRTHDAY WISH TO A FRIEND

By Roy E. Peterson (February 19, 2012)

I wish you more than a special day!
I wish God to wipe any tears away.
His arms reach down to you anywhere
Enfolding you with my birthday prayer.

I wish you a joy filled rest of your life.
Free from pain and free from strife.
A time to rejoice in God's mercy and grace.
A time to savor at a gentle pace.

As gold is sifted from soil refined,
You are the essence of love defined.
We once shared a spark of love sincere,
And intimate nights while I held you near.

I'm supposing our love wasn't meant to be
As we drifted apart. Was it you or me?
Embers still smolder from a word or glance,
But they can't rekindle our past romance.

MY HEART WAS FOOLISH ONCE AGAIN

By Roy E. Peterson (April 2, 2012)

I woke today surprised to find
I had someone on my mind.
I knew her fifty years ago
Perhaps our friendship could regrow.

My heart was foolish once again.
I thought of things that might have been,
If I pursued a different course,
Or would I have the same remorse?

In trepidation I reached out.
I let her know without a doubt
That I was interested in her
And all the things that could infer.

Although another wanted me
It wasn't something meant to be.
I am selective, give me that
She loved her dog I loved my cat.

Since I am living all alone,
I wrote her, "Call me on the phone".
Although I had my reservation
Let's see what happens in conversation.
Perhaps because I'm growing older
That's why I am getting bolder.
In part it's overcoming fears
In part the urgency of years.

I'll tell you in another rhyme
What happened and in time
The key deciders of my fate,
While by the phone I have to wait.

PART XIII

MY THOUGHTS

Monticello Painting

DECISIONS, DECISIONS

By Roy E. Peterson (February 20, 2012)

Be the leader don't follow someone said.
And so the new "leader" came up dead.

Blaze your own trail, don't follow the route.
And so he got lost and stumbled about.

Follow your gut, don't follow directions.
And so the man made no connections.

Follow your wishes, don't follow the crowd.
They buried him alone in a funeral shroud.

Follow your dreams, not some advice.
And so he had to fix it twice.

Question the rules, don't follow them.
That's why man invented the word mayhem.

Do what you love, not what they say.
And so you will pay, and pay, and pay.

Be awesome, not safe, words that sound so good.
And so he was awesome while lost in the woods.

AVOIDING THE ABYSS

By Roy E. Peterson (March 10, 2012)

Everyone passes through life differently.
No one fits the predestined model exactly.
Free will intervenes in the process of perfection.
Environment often determines acceptance or rejection.

Strong will can overcome circumstance and element.
Everyone has potential for deviltry or living testament.
Evil intentioned are not redeemed by one act of kindness.
But one bad decision can result in cultural blindness.

One bad deed can destroy life, liberty, and relations.
We are the product of those around us and our associations.
Except for family, we choose those with whom we share.
Evaluate, caste off those who will drag us down. Select with
        care.

Avoiding the abyss is the essence of wellness and survival
Turning around is the only way of finding self revival.
Drugs, alcohol, and sexual diseases I can tell you surely
Are three paved paths to the inky mists of time prematurely.

Risky behavior including rides in vehicles that are speeding
May result in accidents in which one is at a minimum
        bleeding.
Controlling ourselves is the way to increase our fame.
Discipline and preserving reputation mean everything to our
        name.

EXPLAINING THE UNEXPLAINABLE

By Roy E. Peterson (March 10, 2012)

With trepidation I embark on a torturous quest
To explain some secrets I've kept close to my breast.
Even psychologists cannot clearly explain
The visions and passions that cavort in the brain.

Since I will never undergo the act of hypnosis,
I keep locked away almost every psychosis.
Relatives and friends may have strong fascinations
With delusions of grandeur or my hallucinations.

Now let me explain the unexplainable
How fictionalized accounts are thus attainable.
The contradiction between life lived and observed
And the telling of stories apparently unreserved.

Some secrets one must savor in one's hidden harbor
Safe from judgmental observers forever.
Better the treasure chests of stories n'er told
And keep the locks sealed to protect the gold.

Experiences authors must write unencumbered
Without full disclosure and keep them unnumbered.
Draped on the stories are fantasies imagined
Baring the soul without being burdened.

From the safety of the author's imagination
Words pour out in fictional transformation.
Restrictions that pervade the earthly existence
Are given free flight in ethereal brilliance.

FACEBOOK FEARS

By Roy Eugene Peterson (February 7, 2011)

Sometimes when I grow weary I sit and take a look
At all the friends that matter inhabiting Facebook.
I feel as though intruding, asking pardon for my stare
As I sip my coffee slowly, sitting in my chair.

Is it alright to answer some question that they raise?
What are they really looking for? Some help? A little
  praise?
Sometimes I wish they heard me. I wish there were a mic.
Perhaps just press the button, the one that says I "Like".

Should I write a comment upon their precious wall?
Maybe they don't want me to say anything at all.
I know that if I answer the whole wide world can see
The personal things I say there. What will they think of me?

How did an old acquaintance become a friendly face?
And want to learn about me, through questions on this
  space?
When did the world get closer impinging on my day?
When did I have to carefully prepare the words I say?

For all the world is watching to read just what I write.
Some friend will lol it, while others pick a fight.
But I just want to share some things that show just who I
  am.
A friendly Facebook denizen, perhaps a funny ham.

I'M SORRY I'M NOT PERFECT

By Roy E. Peterson (March 30, 2012)

I truly am not perfect. I really don't know why.
Sometimes I use the bathroom. Sometimes I have to cry.
Sometimes I am forgetful. Sometimes I tell a lie.
I'm sorry I'm not perfect, but Lord knows how I try.

I have to ask forgiveness for half the things I do,
When I have slighted someone, or not worked something
      through.
When I have hurt some feelings, or made a friend feel blue.
I'm sorry I'm not perfect, but I will try anew.

I have to take a bath and have to wash my clothes.
I have to brush my teeth, as any human knows.
I have to watch the words I say and not be one of those.
I'm sorry I'm not perfect, but neither is a rose.

If I have made you angry, the devil's running free.
I'm not sure why I do it. Can we just let it be?
If I forget to help you, or drive you up a tree,
I'm sorry I'm not perfect. I guess it's cause I'm me.

I promise to be better, to watch the things I say.
I promise you true friendship and help you every day.
You know I'll always love you, but my feet are made of clay.
I'm sorry I'm not perfect. But Lord knows how I pray

BAGGAGE

By Roy E. Peterson (December 2011)

Baggage is the guilt we bear
Things that we can never share.
Weights upon our inner core.
Burdens that we keep in store.

Baggage is something we control.
We need to purify the soul.
Get rid of it is my advice.
You have the power to excise.

Get rid of baggage in your lives.
I'm not including former wives.
They are still a part of me
Though they think they set me free.

I thought that we would never part.
I'm romantic in my heart.
Seems they saw it otherwise,
Since they married other guys.

ROSES AND DIRT BAGS

By Roy E. Peterson (March 2012)

I have a rating system for those I love and for those I despise.
A very simple method for delineating values with one
through five.
Five roses is reserved for those most valued in my life.
Five dirt bags for those against whom I will strive.

THE POET AND THE PAINTER: INTROSPECTION

By Roy E. Peterson (April 5, 2102)

I fully understand now how all the poets feel.
They don't know if there's anyone who thinks their thoughts
are real.
A poet to be worth the read must open up their soul
And thoughts for crass inspection; amusement sometimes
cruel.

I remember reading once, "People will talk you know."
They'll comment on the fantasies; dark places that you go
To shed some light of wisdom, or open up the mind.
The common folk will twitter, but they're the ones who're
blind.

A poet is a painter, who uses words for color;
An artist of a special sort, a penitent at the altar;
Observant and romantic; creative; fervent master
Of more than rhyme and reason, a pedant and a crafter.

The paper is the canvas, the desk top is the easel.
The pen in place of paintbrush, the palette is the sepal.
The words evoke the image, as color strikes the senses;
The poet like the artist, in past and present tenses.

Some poets write of shadows. Some poets write of beauty.
Some poets write of history. Some poets write of duty.
Some poets write love sonnets. Some poets, allegory.
Some poets write the world they see. Some poets tell a story.

Beyond the world of senses, the poet paints the dream.
Alternative realities are more than what they seem.
Not everyone can hear them, or taste, or smell, or see,
Or reach out with their mind set; touch unreality.

Some people are afraid it seems, to look within themselves,
To buy a book of poetry to place on dusty shelves.
Although I know some do this, buy Edgar Allan Poe.
A false pretense of intellect is often just for show.

Please let me share a secret. All poets have a need
To feel their work's appreciated like starving artists feed
Upon some kind approval, some passing accolade.
To counter all the ridicule of which they are afraid.

ON GREATNESS

By Roy E. Peterson (April 15, 2012)

It's often hard to recognize
The greatness one exemplifies.
The greatness of a person lies
Within the heart; behind the eyes.

The platinum parent, the friend of gold
It matters not if young or old.
Their greatness may remain untold
Yet somehow they still fit the mold.

A Christian is required first
The Living Water slakes their thirst.
In God's love they are immersed
And real happiness they disbursed.

The greatest have a moral code
They always take the narrow road.
Their inner strength doth not erode.
They always share another's load.

They may be someone near at hand.
A person who will take a stand.
Someone the world may think is bland.
A member of the angel band.

Beauty will fade and muscles too.
Greatness comes from things they do.
Wisdom is another good clue
And patience to see all things through.

The greatest aren't afraid to say
Please watch your step, tread well today.
Take time for God, his word obey,
Or for your sins you'll have to pay.

Look close around you. Cogitate!
Think of someone you believe's great.
Try to follow and emulate.
Study their actions; how they operate.

Love is the binder. It is the glue.
The keystone trait found in so few.
The greatest ones I ever knew
Never said things they thought untrue.

Fame is fleeting and like the sun
It fades from view when day is done.
Great in God's scheme has just begun,
When the course of life they've run.

SOME THINGS DRIVE ME CRAZY

By Roy E. Peterson (April 18, 2012)

Some things drive me crazy, some things cuckoo.
Some drive me wild and then there is you!
At you first you will write in a friendly way,
But then I can't believe what you have to say.

Got up in the morning to do some work.
Read your new email calling me a jerk.
Then I get a message, "Oh, never mind."
According to the latest you are being kind.

Reading your letters, tell you what I found
Much like a pinball I get bounced around.
I'm like the net for your circus act.
I always try to catch you and have learned to react.

Maybe it's the hormones that induce the mood.
Maybe it's the water or some foreign food.
Maybe it's the weather or a strained relation.
Maybe it's the figment of imagination.

"How do I love thee, let me count the ways,"
Like an E. Barrett Browning in a purple haze.
I listen on the phone and read every word
And try not to let on when you are absurd.

Perhaps I should tell you it is only fair
If you're going crazy, I am almost there.
Together we'll laugh and have some fun
Like two crazy people in the noonday sun.

CRUSADER

By Roy E. Peterson (March 2009)

Crusader smite
Infidel blight
In the land of the invader.
Destroy them all
In the hallowed hall.
Expunge the unholy raider.

Fight gallant knight
Set everything right
Dispatch every filthy invader
To a hellish place
And their kind erase
To the very last Saracen raider.

Thy abomination
Suffer ablation.
Eradicate the invader.
Crusaders unite
In this holy fight
Crowning glory kill the raider

Bomb terrorists
Be optimists
Destroy the evil invader
Regardless where
For them prepare
Now you become the Holy Raider.

BOATS AND I DO NOT AGREE

True Events
By Roy E. Peterson (October 25, 2012)

Boats and I do not agree
I will tell you all my story.
When I'm done I'm sure you'll see
You do not want to boat with me.

My college roommate got me to
Go on his dad's boat that was new.
We soon found out he had no clue
About his boat, or what to do.

He headed for the center lake
And laughed at making quite a wake,
His dad was such a big fruitcake
A spare gas can he did not take.

Friends gave him gas. He turned around.
He revved the motor as he wound
It up to max and then he found
He had no brake. We ran aground.

For thirty years I did not go
Upon the boats that I feared so
Until in Russia you must know
I got aboard to my sorrow.

Foreign Service Officer
The title on me did confer
Business facilitator
American company broker

A major firm requested I
Accompany them and with a sigh
I thought my duty was to comply
Besides what things could go awry.

The pilot was the Harbor Master
Pulled the anchor then he cast her
Off the pier and ran it faster
Toward the island and disaster.

In the middle of the bay
When my fears had gone away
The boat hit rock about halfway
A perfect ending for my day.

The drunken pilot climbed about.
"Climb to the rail," he did shout.
"Please give me help to bail it out;
Then we'll continue, I've no doubt."

I had my doubt, I had my fear.
I thought, "What am I doing here?"
After an hour we were clear
With Russkiy Island drawing near.

The last time on a boat it sank
Right next to the island bank.
Who was it that I had to thank
For fishing me out of the tank.

I know that I shall never be
A sailor who will set to sea.
I think that we can all agree
That boating wasn't made for me.

MY PROMISE

By Roy E. Peterson (2010)

I Promise—To give true love to others as the greatest gift
from God,
To live my own life my own way though others think it odd,
To seek improvement of myself though others might
chastise,
And never give myself the time to others criticize.

To give each person I may meet a smile of warmth and not of
pride;
To offer a hand in fellowship where others may deride,
To cultivate new friendships with those who're seeking
mine,
To keep my friends as jewels and not leave them behind.

To keep my strength and inner health so I may be half smart,
That I may have the stamina to finish what I start.
To think the best, to do my best, and expect the best from all
The ones I meet, the things I do, and never hit the wall.

To let nothing hurt my peace of mind and keep my
self-respect,
To consider thoughts that others have, but still be
circumspect.
To forget mistakes that I have made and keep them in the
past,
To remember all the good in life, though it goes by so fast.

To be too big for anger, and optimistic too,
To calm to worry, too strong for fear, too quick for trouble's
brew.
To be faithful in what I do and say; these promises to keep,
Then I need never apologize and get my good night's sleep.

MY PRAYER

By Roy E. Peterson (Unknown Date)

O' give us love for all mankind
And help us overcome
The evil forces of this world
In love, "Thy will be done."

I am your sword of vengeance
And instrument of might
To destroy the evil ones
And win in any fight.

ADVICE FROM MARINE COLONELS

By Roy E. Peterson (2011)

A Marine Corps Colonel once told me
Never issue an apology.
I heard his words and I agree
All's fair in war and liberty.

He told me, son please stop explaining
You're losing and you are nothing gaining.
Remember you're winning if you're refraining
From causing doubt by your complaining.

In Garmisch I lived across the hall
When down below we heard Jonathan bawl.
In a deep echo voice I heard him call.
This is God! Shut up! And that was all.

Another Marine Colonel changed my vision
The Soviets can't create a new division.
Only God creates and it's His decision.
Now please rewrite your presentation.

A Marine Jet Pilot had in his den
A photo with words from way back when.
There they go I must hurry after them
For I am their leader and they are my men.

LOOKING FOR YOUR SANITY

**(Response to Facebook item from Craig Adams:
"If you find my sanity, send it home to me.")
By Roy E. Peterson (October 29, 2012)**

I started looking for your sanity
So I could send it back to you.
I began looking in my vanity,
But my drawers were empty too.

I checked my desk and bookshelf
And my computer as last resort.
Then I checked the kitchen myself
But still had nothing to report.

I checked with friends on Facebook
But found you were not alone.
They were looking for who took
Their own sanity from their home.

The world has gone to pieces
No more sanity to be found.
The politicians and their speeches
Sent sanity underground.

VAMPIRES OF NEW ENGLAND

By Roy E. Peterson (November 1, 2012)

The vampires of New England, if you believe the scuttlebutt
Ranged from Salem, Massachusetts to Griswold,
Connecticut.
Even in Rhode Island, there's a town named Exeter
Where graves were opened later and bodies would
disappear.

Exhumations were quite common as people there were led
To open up the coffins and disarticulate the head.
Up to the year of nineteen hundred, superstitions there
abound.
Townsfolk blamed the evil demons and the vampires
underground.

I will give you one example dated eighteen fifty four
When the Jewett City townsfolk no longer could ignore
The legends of the vampires arising from their graves.
So they dug up all the bodies and pierced their hearts with
staves.

Often the local parson was made to perform the rite
To ward off evil demons in a clandestine affair at night.
One vampire heart in Woodstock, Vermont it's said was
scorched
In a ritual in eighteen thirty, on the public square was
torched.

In Manchester hundreds gathered at a blacksmith's place one
night
In seventeen hundred ninety-three to ward off demon fright.
Timothy Mead officiated to burn hearts in sacrifice
To a blood sucking Vampire Demon and hoped that would
suffice.

The townsfolk who called the meeting said they were very certain
Vampires still were sucking blood from the wife of Captain Burton.
The townsfolk bowed to Satan and they all began to praying.
The history of the town says it was winter and good sleighing

Exeter's most famous vampire was a lass named Mercy Brown
Who at the tender age of nineteen severely vexed the town.
Her family called her Lena. The townsfolk called her trash.
So they burned her heart to cinders and made her brother eat the ash.

On Halloween hooded figures still make a pilgrimage
Through the swamp oak and the maple most of them just teenage.
Park the car at Chestnut Hill there in the Baptist parking lot.
The church still uses the grave sites, but there you'll find her plot.

What is left of Lena is buried in the Chestnut cemetery.
Old-timers don't like the pilgrims. If you go you must be wary.
A year or two ago teenagers died on Purgatory Road
That leads up to the grave site just a day before it snowed.

The lichen claims the tombstones of most who're buried there.
But then you'll see one gravestone that is showing very clear.
The marker has low value, but the pilgrims give it worth.
You will find it strapped with iron, firmly anchored to the earth.

What explains belief in vampires and their earthly
depredation?
The people of New England lived in cultural isolation.
They were a largely heathen lot despite the reputation
Of New Englander's puritanical religious affiliation.

In place of organized religion, superstitions ruled the land.
Only ten percent church goers, let the rest get out of hand.
Magic springs with healing powers, dead bodies that still
bled
Fed their warped imagination with the wicked at the head.

Shoes were placed next to the chimney to catch the devil if he
tried
To enter through the fireplace and try to get inside.
Nailed horseshoes over door frames and carved out daisy
wheels,
A colonial kind of hex sign that their fear surely reveals.

To a frantic population a kinsman owed it to the town
To quell their fear of vampires by letting them dig down
Into the grave that held their kinfolk and then leave him
alone,
After they had torn the heart out and replaced it with a
stone.

VELVET HAMMER

By Roy E. Peterson (November 5, 2012)

A velvet hammer is the fuzzy striker of a string
Inside piano sound boxes to make the pure note ring.
Though it is soft and velvety it amplifies the sound.
When keyboard notes are hit hard, they loudly will resound.

A second definition uses an orange or coffee taste liqueur.
When mixed with cream and vodka, it can make the senses
blur.
The drink consumed is softened and does not burn the
throat,
But when you've had too many, you'll feel your body float.

Let me explain the meaning in a way you'll understand.
A velvet hammer is someone or something that seems bland.
It quietly sneaks up on you and softly will engage.
You'll never know what hit you, but can do major damage.

A colleague in a military classroom gave me the nickname,
The "Velvet Hammer" for the way I put the rest to shame.
I'd listen to their arguments and then take it apart.
They never saw it coming as I then ripped out their heart.

I am the Velvet Hammer. I accept the moniker.
I'll win the final argument and others will concur
You didn't see it coming. You stepped into my trap.
Every point you made in arguing fell right into my lap.

DOGGEREL DAYS

By Roy E. Peterson (November 14, 2012)

I found no Facebook coffee poster.
I found no email person roaster.
Wednesday is a no call day.
Nothing left for you to say?

I know that I may be erratic.
And I sometimes am ecstatic
Just to take a day or two
Off before I then respond to you.

But you are of another sort.
Always ready to report.
Loyal, patient, communicator.
Conversation facilitator.

I hope your headache's gone away
That you mentioned yesterday.
I hope you have no pain or loss
And that you lightly bear your "cross".

Did they repair your breaker box?
Did you get to wash your socks?
I hope your leg's not sore today
And that the pain has gone away.

ME, MY BOSS, AND CORRESPONDING LADY FRIEND

By Roy E. Peterson (April 18, 2012)

Up, but hopefully not for the day.
My boss called early just to say
Typical problems in La La Land.
He was writing a letter with his hand.

The next thing I knew I heard a shout
Cursed the lawyer walking about.
A favorite reaction, but not at me.
I was thinking, just let it be.

For an hour I was tired as heck.
Wanted to wring his stupid neck
I'd take a hammer to his head.
And watch night time TV instead.

He told me early in the morn
Type a letter without things sworn.
He asked me to send them on my own
Then call him on the telephone.

Now I must guess what he would say;
Prepared the letter anyway.
Watched three shows then went to bed;
Thoughts of the letter stuck in my head.

Schedule erratic. When can I sleep.
Sometimes instantly counting sheep.
Read your emails now and then,
But when can I answer, tell me when.

Your timing's off as much as mine.
Now you're drawing a new line,
Each day I sent you an email
And answered to you without fail.

Guess not enough to listen to you,
Or read about all the things you do.
Thought you needed someone to hear,
Who thought that you were precious dear.

I accomplished most everything
On my list for self publishing.
Vow that today it will be done
Sometime before the setting sun.

My boss believes in testament;
Preparing a court worthy document.
In case we take someone to trial,
When we have money, after awhile.

Now back to work write and research
It's Sunday and I'm missing church.
Have to read lots of emails sent.
Quote from them all and do not vent.

Spent forty-five minutes to send to you
A more worthy email; sad but true.
What possesses me at 2 AM?
Hope not a demon. One of them!

PATIENCE IS A VIRTUE

By Roy E. Peterson (November 15, 2012)

Patience is a virtue. Or so says some soothesayer.
Though you have not heard from me, you're always in my prayer.
If you can't feel the power that frizzes up your hair,
It doesn't mean I'm callous or that I just don't care.

Though patience is a virtue, you really must decide
If it is worth the time spent, or if somebody lied.
Just ask the patient fisherman who silently will wait
Beside a brook or river for fish to take the bait.

I think that fish were put on earth as a utility
To train men to be patient and learn humility.
The women too were given a patience learning tool,
A man for them to practice on whether smart or whether fool.

A person with no patience may cause an accident.
They'll double up the time that they already spent.
The damage that they're doing may be irreparable.
They take the hand of danger and become inseparable.

Thus I would counsel patience to seek reality.
Expectations crumble upon your vanity.
Just realize that others have many things to do,
And when their tasks are finished, they'll get back to you.

If you want to know the reason some people have success,
It's a dose of pure persistence combined with their patience.
As Leo Tolstoy stated, "The strongest warriors are these two:
Time and patience" coupled with desire to see it through.

TREASURES IN HEAVEN

By Roy E. Peterson (October 30, 2012)

I am not laying up treasures in heaven.
I don't expect a star for a crown.
I only want to be there with Jesus
And touch the hem of his royal white gown.

Don't need a palace or even a mansion.
I don't desire some manna to eat.
Just let me share the presence of Jesus;
One moment to sit right next to his feet.

Our mind cannot grasp the world that is heaven.
Words can't convey such magnificence.
Who can conceive the glory of Jesus?
Basking in love next to his presence.

It's fun to think of treasures in heaven.
It's fun to think of streets of pure gold.
The treasure is there, but not as we think it.
It's sharing the story that never grows old.

I know when I die that I'm bound for heaven
You may think of it as a beautiful city.
But let me lie down beside the still waters,
Where I can live for eternity.

ODE TO THE NARCISSIST

By Roy E. Peterson (November 25, 2012)

The narcissist was captivated
By the things she had created.
To herself she thus related
Images she cultivated.

The narcissist broke every mirror,
Because her image should be clearer.
She could never understand
Why others did not think her grand.

There must be some deficiency
If others could not her agree.
The image that she did create?
The world is small, but I am great.

LOVE AT LOST LAKE

By Roy E. Peterson (November 25, 2012)

New-na-new-new and Tra La La La.
Shho Bee Do Do and Sha Na Na Na.
I remember Doo Wop Wop;
Drifters at the Olde Malt Shoppe.
Coasters playing on the box.
Platters softly singing rock.
New-na-new-new and Tra La La La.
Shho Bee Do Do and Sha Na Na Na.

Ring-a-ding-dong, Ling-a-ling-long.
Ram-a-ding-dong, Sing-a-sing-song.
Met my date on Friday night.
Rocking music out of sight.
Held my baby close to me.
Held our kiss to count of three.
Ring-a-ding-dong, Ling-a-ling-long.
Ram-a-ding-dong, Sing-a-sing-song.

Bom-a-bom-bom, Do-do-do-do.
Lom-a-lom-lom, Shu-shu-shu-shu.
Took my date to the picture show.
Drive-in theater parked last row.
Couldn't see the picture screen.
Too much kissing, too much steam.
Bom-a-bom-bom, Do-do-do-do.
Lom-a-lom-lom, Shu-shu-shu-shu.

Kom-a, kom, kom and Be Bop-a Lula.
Shoma, lom, lom and Boola-bo-boola.
Then we drove to our lost lake.
Where our loving we would make.
Had to get home before ten.
If we did, we could go again.
Kom-a, kom, kom and Be Bop-a Lula.
Shoma, lom, lom and Boola-bo-boola

THE ICE CREAM TRUCK

By Roy E. Peterson (Started June/Finished November 2012)

The Ice Cream Truck in June
Still plays a Christmas tune.
I shouldn't be upset,
But it's not Christmas yet.
I think I'll buy a float
And cram it down his throat.
And then just for the heck of it
I'll just stand back and gloat.

Chorus:
Oh, Ice Cream Truck, Ice Cream Truck
Why have you run amuck.
Find some other music now
For you are out of luck.
Ice Cream Truck, Ice Cream Truck
You get off my street,
Or find some other music now
And change your stupid beat.

It's been almost a year
And Christmas time is near.
For now no need to fear;
I wish you Christmas cheer,
But after New Year's Day
You better stay away.
If you know what is good for you,
New tunes you better play.

I went to buy a pop
The truck just wouldn't stop.
The driver drove along
Just playing that same song.
I went to get my gun
The children tried to run
But they could not catch up with him
And so the kids got none.

I think he drove through here
While drinking lots of beer.
He didn't want to sell
This Ice Cream Truck from hell.
So I called up his boss
And told him of his loss
The driver was replaced and now
There is no more chaos.

MY LITTER BOX

By Roy E. Peterson (December 3, 2012)

I found I have a litter box and don't know what to do.
It wasn't made for dogs or cats, yet they come into view.
They call it social media. Please write upon my wall.
Please post a picture of your kids, or dogs, or cats and all.

My litter box is filled each day with cryptic messages,
Photo stills, and statement frames, and inane passages.
I yearn for something special with originality,
Instead I get, "What do you think of my frivolity?"

The women love the babies, their gossip, and their views,
Their kitty cats and puppies complete with barks and mews.
The men don't write as often; perhaps about a sport;
And they don't flood my inbox when there's nothing to report.

Some want to be the first one to propagate the news
And add their own impressions and tell of their own views.
Some love to spread the gossip, "Say did you hear the one . . ."
Just like in my old high school days, the grapevine's never done.

We all seek validation, approval from our peers.
We all like adulation and getting hugs and cheers.
But some need constant feedback a hundred times a day.
For all the things they're thinking and everything they say.

If I should dare to send a post, I try for something new.
The items that I write each day are only one or two.
I try to think each posting through and try not to abuse
The privilege of my sharing and hope I can amuse.

It can be overwhelming, the volume of my mail.
The clicker diarrhea could make my system fail.
At least with new controllers I remove them from my feed.
And relegate offenders to the "maybe I will read."

Some people need attention, some people need a friend.
Some think they must report on the latest social trend.
Some think they are important and that we need to hear
Their take on social consciousness, or problems that they fear.

The problem is I like my friends and don't want to delete.
The system says I could "unfriend," but sometimes they are neat.
I often search for something good, for something I can use,
But waste a lot of time in searching through their old refuse.

Sometimes I find a nugget hidden somewhere in their trash,
But then they fill my inbox with the issues they rehash.
Peripatetic senders have all become a ghost
Existing in my friend file, removed from daily post.

I find that less is better. It makes my focus clear.
A word of wit or wisdom, of humor and good cheer.
I strive to be creative, to think of something new.
And not be like a hurricane with winds that just blew threw.

I navigate the channels of my social intercourse
Consider all my options and then consider source.
I need to find the beacon to keep me off the rocks
To stop the vessel sinking from the stuff in my inbox.

So if you read this message, stop sending so much junk.
Reduce the flow of "do you know" and keep it in your trunk.
Although you think you're wiser and need to educate,
When you choose to litter, no way can one relate.

DICKENS ON THE STRAND

By Roy E. Peterson (December 1, 2012)
Inspired by Moody Garden Lights in Galveston and
mention of the annual "Dickens on the Strand".

If Charles Dickens you see on the Strand
With *Oliver Twist* and the *Copperfield* Band,
Tell him that Scrooge is still happy at last
With no further visits from ghosts of the past.

His *Christmas Carol* I watch on tv,
While drinking eggnog and trimming the tree.
Tell him the lessons I seek to apply
And Tiny Tim still brings a tear to my eye.

A Tale of Two Cities in high school I read.
And the Old Curiosity Shop is not dead.
With *Great Expectations* I hope I may see
The lights of the garden once owned by Moody.

PART XIV

ANIMAL CRACKERS

Peaceable Kingdom Painting by Edward Hicks

IF I WERE AN ANIMAL, WHICH ONE WOULD I BE?

By Roy E. Peterson (April 4, 2012)

If I were an animal, where would I be?
Down on the ground or up in a tree?
Perhaps in the sky flying in a vee?
Or swimming around down under the sea?

If I were an animal, how would I hide?
Perhaps in a burrow where I could abide.
A good camouflage I sure would have tried.
Or hidden myself down under the tide.

If I were an animal, what could I do
So I could avoid the fate of a zoo?
Run faster than wind, fly high in the air?
Use razor sharp claws, or have teeth that can tear?

If I were an animal, who would I be?
A soft Teddy Bear, so soft and snuggly.
With a mistress to carry me under her arm
To hug me a lot and keep me from harm.

BADGER, BADGER

By Roy E. Peterson (August 8, 2012)

Badger, Badger, crafty soul.
Are you hiding in your hole?
Or are you lurking in the night
Where the bonfire's burning bright.

Maybe you are underground
In hidden safety without sound.
Maybe you are hunting meat
Daggers from your claw filled feet.

Though your sighting's rather rare,
All the others must beware.
They cannot get close to you
Fearful of the things you do.

It may be hard to understand,
How you can live your life as planned.
Protector of your family;
Provider most uncannily.

Fiercely loyal, powerful, brave
In the woods or in your cave.
Band of brothers you respect
And other badgers you protect.

Badgers are a special breed.
They help each other when in need.
Support in spirit where ere they are
Whether near or whether far.

MY NEIGHBOR'S DOG

By Roy E. Peterson (October 28, 2012)

My neighbor's dog is very rude. He always barks at me.
And what could be the use of him is more than I can see.
He cannot scale my six foot fence although I know he tried.
I can tell he jumps and lands still on the other side.

I have a good solution that should not be too hard.
I'll simply buy a tiger and put him in my yard.
One bark is all that I should hear, just one final yap
And I'd release the tiger from the tiger trap.

No more doggie barking! I'd have peace at last.
It soon would be all over. I'm sure it would be fast.
I have one little problem. It may not be a snap
To get my roving tiger back in the tiger trap.

SEATTLE SLEW

By Roy E. Peterson (October 29, 2012)

I never saw a race horse
Run like he would do.
He'd fall behind the others
You thought that he was through.

Then somewhere on the back stretch
The horse would start to run
Much like a bullet speeding
From the muzzle of a gun.

He'd pass the fainting fillies
And stallions on the way
To win another horse race
And take the prize that day.

Could it have been the jockey
Or the trainer and his crew?
Whatever, he was exciting.
The horse? Seattle Slew.

BEES

With a nod to Joyce Kilmer (*Trees*)
By Roy E. Peterson (November 14, 2012)

I think that I shall never see
An insect better than a bee.

A bee whose sticky legs are prest
Against the flower's pollen breast.

A bee that flies around all day
Collecting pollen on its way.

A bee that may in summer wear
A coat of pollen on its hair.

Upon whose bosom when 'tis sunny
Depends the making of the honey.

Poems are made by fools like me,
But only God can make a bee.

YOU AT THE ZOO

By Roy E. Peterson (November 16, 2012)

Said the monkey at the zoo
You have something more to do.
Buy some peanuts at the stand;
Put them in my little hand.

Said the tiger behind bars
You should thank your lucky stars
You are not in here with me,
While I'm feeling this hungry.

Said the laughing hyena
I could tell you my saga
How I once was running free
Now you see the joke's on me.

Said the panda eating bamboo
I am thankful for the zoo.
If it weren't for such a place
I'd have no more living space.

Said the panther I agree
The zoo's a better place for me.
There's no jungle left out there.
In the wild my kind is rare.

Don't be sorry. Don't feel blue
For the animals in the zoo.
Thank the world for each zoo park.
Think of them as Noah's Ark.

ANIMAL CRACKERS

Why No One Wants Me to Write a Nursery Rhyme
By Roy E. Peterson (November 17, 2012)

How now you stupid cow.
No more milk you will allow?
I'll have your head, I'll have your hide
Then eat the meat you keep inside.

Bow wow you doggy dow
If you keep barking at the cow,
I'll get my gun. You better run
And then we'll see who's having fun.

Quack, quack you ducky hack.
Who took the manners that you lack?
What's your appeal? A Christmas meal
Is how I'm going to seal the deal.

Cluck, cluck you chicken pluck.
I think you're running out of luck.
When I am able, I will ladle
Gravy on you from my table.

Grunt, grunt you hog up front.
I'm going to put it to you blunt—
I want your pork stuck on my fork.
Now guess who they will call a dork.

Meyew, meyew you catty crew
I wonder what you cats can do.
Your fate is grim. I have a whim.
I wonder if you cats can swim.

Mouse, mouse I told my spouse
I think a mouse is in the house.
I set a trap and took a nap
Until I heard the wire snap.

My farm is neat and growing wheat.
No animals are left to greet.
The corn grows high and so am I
In maize and barley, flax and rye.

IF I RAN THE RODEO

By Roy E. Peterson (November 17, 2012)

If I ran the rodeo,
'Twould be a very different show.
Girls dressed in lingerie
Would surely take men's breath away.

Some would be bikini clad
And show us everything they had.
The ropers with their good lasso
Would soon corral the pretty crew.

Young Indian maidens dancing nude
Would appeal to every dude.
What a vision! What a chance
To watch them do a native dance.

The barrel ride would be more fun
The men could watch them naked run
Their horses in a figure eight.
I think that would be really great.

Bareback riding in the nude
Soon would have the men unglued.
Every man within the town
Would want to be the rodeo clown.

MY PERFECT PET

By Roy E. Peterson (November 24, 2012)

I remember in the seventies I bought the perfect pet.
It did not cost a lot and I think I have him yet.
He came with full instructions in a tiny little box.
The name I gave was Mister Stone and he was my pet rock.

Some tricks he knew already, commands like sit and stay.
But others were a problem, like roll over in the hay.
He never interrupted me when I would watch a game
And in a conversation he listened just the same.

I never had to feed him or make him take a bath.
For grins I introduced him to the rocks along the path.
I trusted him to stay at home and never make a mess.
He never showed emotion and he never caused me stress.

I never made him wear a leash and never tied him up.
I could put him on the table next to my coffee cup.
The cost of care and maintenance was nothing, it was free.
So why would cats and dogs be kept is more than I could see.